"Simply in a league of its own! Building on her ground-breaking *Jung in India*, Sengupta makes a stellar contribution to the cultural revision – and hence renaissance – of Jungian theory and practice. It is one of the most important de-colonisations in the entire field of depth psychology and psychoanalysis. Everyone will benefit, in the West too. Of particular importance is the interweave of mythology and contemporary crises in India. After this work, we cannot look at contra-sexuality, and especially at the animus, in an unchanged way."

Professor Andrew Samuels, author of *The Political Psyche*

"Through her incisive and compassionate twenty-first century feminist lens, Sulagna Sengupta's *Animus, Psyche and Culture,* takes C. G. Jung's controversial masculine other and makes it into the most searching and revelatory lens on culture and gender in India. This is Transdisciplinary Jungian research at its most creative and empowering. *Animus, Psyche and Culture* blends depth psychology, Jung, post-Jungian scholarship, myth, film, religion and history for astonishing insights that put the animus forefront in thinking about culture and psyche. The book provides a vivid and compelling argument evaluating the tangle of gender, power, vision and individuation."

Susan Rowland (PhD) is core faculty at Pacifica Graduate Institute and author of *Jung: A Feminist Revision* (2002), and with Joel Weishaus, *Jungian Arts-Based Research and the Nuclear Enchantment of New Mexico* (2021)

"A remarkable reworking and re-visioning of Jung's views on the counter-sexual other in the psyche, especially with regards to the experience of women. This is a work for the 21st century, advancing analytical psychology through expertly chosen personal and cultural reflections on patterns of gendering. Sulagna Sengupta, an acclaimed cultural historian in Jungian studies, here opens up fertile paths for exploring gender fluidity while carefully respecting and articulating cultural differences. This well-researched text is a virtual banquet of Jungian and post-Jungian thought, contemporizing and bringing renewed relevance to a subject that had been submerged by past critiques. The presentation is richly storied and emancipatory, pioneering transdisciplinary principles in the study of culture and unconscious processes."

Joe Cambray, PhD, Past-President/CEO, Pacifica Graduate Institute

"Sulagna Sengupta's offers a rich phenomenological description of the animus in its many aspects, through a series of narratives in the context of

Indian culture. She rightly underlines the importance of culture in the formation of the contra-sexual other. In doing so, she corrects the tendency to consider the animus one-sidedly as a merely subjective inner factor with fixed meanings, that reflect traditional gender assumptions. Through a discussion of the ideas of post-Jungian authors and Jung's own position on the animus, Sengupta offers a stimulating and convincing revision of Jung's views. The animus appears as an individuating life-force, which animates feminine journeys and facilitates creative endeavors in environmental activism, science, invention and writing."

Paul Brutsche, PhD, author of *Creativity- Patterns of Creative Imagination as Seen Through Art*

ANIMUS, PSYCHE AND CULTURE

Animus, Psyche and Culture takes Carl Jung's concept of contra-sexual psyche and locates it within the cultural expanse of India, using ethnographic narratives, history, religion, myth, films, biographical extracts to deliberate on the feminine in psychological, social and archetypal realms.

Jung's concept of unconscious contra-sexuality, based on notions of feminine Eros and masculine Logos, was pioneering in his time, but took masculine and feminine to be fixed and essential attributes of gender in the psyche. This book explores the relevance of the animus, examining its rationale in current contexts of gender fluidity. Taking off from Post Jungian critiques, it proposes an exposition of the animus in history, social and religious phenomena, theories of knowledge, psychoid archetype and synchronicity, to grasp its nuances in diverse cultural worlds. This study re-envisions the notion of animus keeping in mind the intricacies of feminine subjectivity and the diversity of cultural worlds where depth psychological ideas are currently emerging.

A remarkable reworking of Jungian ideas, this well-researched and important new book will be an insightful read for Jungian analysts and scholars with an interest in cultural and gender studies.

Sulagna Sengupta is a Jungian scholar and cultural historian based in Bangalore, India. She is the author of *Jung in India (2013)* and other writings. Her website is www.Jung-India.org

ANIMUS, PSYCHE AND CULTURE

A Jungian Revision

Sulagna Sengupta

Routledge
Taylor & Francis Group

LONDON AND NEW YORK

Designed cover image: © Boisali Biswas

First published 2024
by Routledge
4 Park Square, Milton Park, Abingdon, Oxon OX14 4RN

and by Routledge
605 Third Avenue, New York, NY 10158

Routledge is an imprint of the Taylor & Francis Group, an informa business

© 2024 Sulagna Sengupta

British Library Cataloguing-in-Publication Data
A catalogue record for this book is available from the British Library

ISBN: 978-1-138-38974-8 (hbk)
ISBN: 978-1-138-38976-2 (pbk)
ISBN: 978-0-429-42372-7 (ebk)

DOI: 10.4324/9780429423727

Typeset in Sabon
by MPS Limited, Dehradun

For Isa

CONTENTS

'Xipe Totec'.

Source: Original artwork by Boisali Biswas.

FIGURES

TABLES

ACKNOWLEDGEMENTS

Cover art: Boisali Biswas

PREFACE

An inquiry on culture, psyche and contra-sexual animus has many implications, especially when there are few depth psychological studies with focus on gender and culture. Also, there has been very little inquiry on culture and psyche with reference to Carl Jung's history with India. Jung's links with India and the notion of 'Cultural Other' are therefore intrinsic to this work. This volume locates Jung's concept of contra-sexual psyche in narratives of culture and uses this to elaborate on the notion of contra-sexuality. It opens up questions about universalist theories of the unconscious, the place of culture in psyche and the relevance of archetypes in cross-cultural enquiries. But more importantly, this work re-envisions the concept of the animus in culture and explores nuances of feminine subjectivity.

In current paradigms of gender fluidity and sexual ambivalence, the notion of contra-sexual opposites may be a tenuous one, especially when masculine and feminine are not viewed as fixed attributes tied to biological gender. In this work, they have been used to denote fixed and dogmatic notions of gender, that are active in culture. The animus brings up the notion of the other, and a psychological attitude that is outside conformist feminine behavior. The constellation of the animus forms the crux of our deliberations on contra-sexuality. This study uses narratives, myths, symbols, history, religion, cultural theories and contemporary Jungian perspectives to explore lived experiences of the feminine, with particular reference to India.

Chapter 1 sets the tone of the volume by contextualizing Jung's ideas in India. It elaborates on the notion of 'Cultural Other', deconstructs archetypes and discusses tensions of race and culture in the Jungian field.

It locates the notion of psyche in a discursive realm of culture and history, and in postcolonial critiques. The significance of cultural journeys in fomenting knowledge, as well as the psychological complexities that these journeys evoke, are highlighted. This chapter shows how gender shapes the process of meaning-making in culture. It also introduces narratives as a tool for articulating feminine subjectivity.

Chapter 2 recounts a dream, the genesis of this book, and locates it in Jung's notion of synchronicity. It delves into the concept of animus and post-Jungian critiques of the concept. It discusses Jung's disconnect from historical realities of gender and suggests a transdisciplinary approach in discoursing contra-sexual psyche. Drawing from Jung's own experience of India, this chapter highlights the importance of having a cultural ground in studying the unconscious animus.

Chapter 3 takes a well-known case from India and examines the phenomenon of rape, viewing feminine subjectivity from contrasting standpoints of archetypal, cultural and psychosocial. It looks at the transformative potential of the contra-sexual archetype and its intricate links in both personal and collective. The multiplicity of the animus, revealed in the narratives, differs from Jung's fixed and linear views about gender. This chapter explores the archetype of phallic feminine in deliberating on the animus.

Chapter 4 takes discrete narrative strands, from myth of the goddess to stories of indigenous and subaltern groups, in diverse frames of inner and outer, to deliberate on sexuality, class, caste, gender and psyche. The phenomenon of the animus is central in these storylines, showing the individuating impulse of the contra-sexual psyche, its agency and independence.

Chapter 5 looks at the phenomenon of synchronicity, or spontaneous events that align unrelated entities and objects meaningfully. Examples of acausal coincidences in wider cultural phenomena, points toward synchronicities constellated in the collective. This chapter outlines the distinctness of Indian thought and Jungian psychology, through a recapitulation of the history of the unconscious. It suggests cultural synchronicity as a ground for the convergence of discrete domains – Jung and India. In contrast to Jung's empirical notions, this chapter relates a Vedic myth and archaic allusions of the animus in culture. It argues that a re-envisioning of the animus needs to include historical differences, social and cultural particulars and the diversity of knowledge across east and west. The animus is conceptualized in this chapter in archaic symbolization, in theories of myth, history, as well as empirical precepts.

Chapter 6 looks at individuation, Jung's concept of life stages and the Indian theological concept of *ashrama*, highlighting how Indian thought is analogous to Jung's ideas, but distinct from them. Their comparative value reiterates the importance of viewing the phenomenon of animus in a broader cultural framework. This chapter explores religious metaphors in viewing a contemporary feminine narrative, finding archetypal and synchronistic elements in its emergence. It suggests that contra-sexual archetypes can be viewed both in personal and objective realms and has significance for healing and cultural revival.

The conclusion looks at the multiplicity of feminine experience and psyche's deep and expansive links in personal, cultural, historical and archetypal realms. It restates the importance of viewing psychological ideas in wider histories and cultural particulars, alongside individual psychology. The phenomenology of the animus shows its creative and disruptive properties. A view of Jung's notion of the animus and its amplification in culture shows that there are significant facets of the archetype that are discernible in feminine histories, and that Jung's theory of contra-sexuality needs to include wider frameworks of knowledge, in deliberating on its psychological nuances.

A few words about the cover image and the artist. Boisali Biswas is a contemporary mixed media artist based in Michigan, USA, whose artwork forms the book's cover. Boisali created the Xipe Totec figurine from scraps of fiber and burlap 20 years ago, inspired by ancient Aztec fertility gods, and left it unattended for some time. When the image spoke to her several years later, she transformed it with leftover material, giving it new life and exhibiting it for juried shows. Boisali is an award-winning artist, with a multi-cultural training in fine arts. I came across Boisali's work quite by chance, through a synchronistic occurrence, and discovered later that she had studied at Visva-Bharati, Rabindranath Tagore's university, around the same time that I had been there. We had, in fact, lived in the same boarding house on the university campus, but had never met. Boisali's creative techniques and aesthetic principles resonate powerfully with the theme of this book and underscore cross-cultural resonance in myth, art and psyche. The Aztec god Xipe Totec, a god of fertility, death and rebirth, has both male and female incarnations. The image shows an androgynous figure, imbued with mana potency. The contra-sexual animus is similarly formed out of many-sided oppositions between inner and outer, in a dialectical psyche. Boisali's art embraces 'the other' in her multifaceted inspirations, use of mixed techniques, and reanimation of an indigenous symbol in contemporary idiom. It reflects the way the concept of the animus has been deliberated in this volume, through diverse cultural histories and knowledge traditions. It is a privilege to have Boisali's work as part of the book's cover.

I have many people to thank for this book. Friends and family who have been with me on my journey, colleagues who have contributed to my growth and my analyst, with whom I have walked a long road. I also thank those who make it possible for me to work every day, helping me sustain an organic life-system – they are intrinsic to this work. I thank Andrew Samuels for envisioning a Jungian-Indian writing, and Routledge for their patience and support.

Sulagna Sengupta, Bangalore

1

INTRODUCTION

The Place of Culture

This chapter foregrounds culture, as a prelude to a discussion on the animus. The psychological phenomenon of the animus is viewed not in psyche's interiority alone, but also in its interaction with a social world. The human environment, its people, history, politics, religion, science and art, evoke in us, notions of a collective. This volume explores the dynamics of unconscious contra-sexuality in the lived experience of a collective. The diversity of social worlds renders gender with widely different nuances across cultures. The structuring principle of the archetype helps in understanding these nuances. The animus is an archetypal construct for understanding unconscious contra-sexual behavior in the psyche. This chapter shows how differences in culture render archetypes with vastly different meanings, and how narratives reveal these differences under their implicit universality. Carl Jung's history with India is central to this work. Jung's reactions to culture in his interactions with India, and his notions about race and gender in general, bring the 'other' into focus. The phenomenon of the animus is explored, keeping in view the notion of the other in psyche and culture.

> At one pole of my being I am one with stocks [sic] and stones. There I have to acknowledge the rule of universal law. That is where the foundation of my existence lies, deep down below. Its strength lies in its being held firm in the clasp of comprehensive world, and in the fullness of its community with all things.

DOI: 10.4324/9780429423727-1

But at the other pole of my being I am separate from all. There I have broken through the cordon of equality and stand alone as an individual. I am absolutely unique, I am I, I am incomparable. The whole weight of the universe cannot crush out this individuality of mine. I maintain it in spite of the tremendous gravitation of all things. It is small in appearance but great in reality. For it holds its own against the forces that would rob it of its distinction and make it one with the dust.

— Rabindranath Tagore, Sadhana: *The Realization of Life,*
The Problem of Self, 1913

Indian poet-philosopher Rabindranath Tagore's (1861–1941) deliberations on self and the world seem close to Swiss psychoanalyst Carl Jung's (1875–1961) notion of individuation. In *Two Essays on Analytical Psychology,* Jung described that outer and inner realities need to be held in balance, with neither condition accommodated exclusively in psychic adaptation (Jung, 1966, para. 240). This view resonates with Tagore's idea of the 'superstructure of the self', wherein the individual balances the weight of the universe against the self, because the self, if lost, is a loss to the world. Tagore deliberated on the notion of self teleologically, comparing it to a seed that sprouts into its own, becomes a tree and finds its relation to all things far and near, in a self-actualization process, that is inherently in tension with universal laws (Tagore, 2019, pp. 47–57).

Jung's idea of the Self, integral to his notion of individuation, describes how the individual becomes a separate, indivisible whole, by rejecting conformity with others. Non-conformity with the collective evokes *tragic guilt* in the individual, which is compensated by a new value or attitude brought back to the collective, in return for what has been rejected. During analysis, for instance, the individual's feelings of resistance towards the analyst is an attitude of non-conformity that affirms the process of individuation (Jung, 1969b, para. 489). Jung emphasized the centrality of the individual and its tensions with the collective as integral to individuation. Individuation is a psychological necessity in which, the superior force of the collective as well as the delicate nature of individuality had to be balanced. (Jung, 1966, para. 241).

Even though Jung's and Tagore's ideas seem identical, Tagore made no reference to the 'psychological' unconscious in his writings. He described unconscious as ignorance or *avidya,* and used Upanishadic ideas of unity and dualism to explain the dialectics of the self. He deliberated that the self was dual, both real and transcendent, material and spiritual, and the experience of selfhood comes from harmonizing these dualities (Tagore, 2019, pp. 56–58). For Jung, the self was made up of conscious and unconscious elements. It signified psychological wholeness, but its nature was indeterminable, as it had aspects of the unconscious psyche (Jung, 1953, para. 20). The distinction between the two viewpoints is critical, as also their differing schools of thought. It shows how perspectives of selfhood are distinct across cultures, and a mechanistic adoption of Jung's ideas in India is detrimental to both analytical psychology and Indian thought. It also suggests why the phenomenon of animus has to take into account specific contexts of culture, diverse traditions of knowledge and actual lived experience, to assimilate its complex nuances and significance.

It was in a series of lectures delivered at Harvard University in 1913 on consciousness and realization of the infinite (compiled later into a book of essays titled *Sadhana*, extracted above) that Tagore deliberated on the self, around the time when Jung himself formulated the notion of individuation in 1915–1916. The parallel is striking, as also the contrasts. Jung's ideas came from his training in psychiatry and his intellectual roots in European philosophy, while Tagore's thoughts were rooted in literary and philosophical tenets of ancient India, a civilization later colonized. Jung and Tagore never met, but both had shared interests in German classicism. In 1908, inspired by Goethe, Tagore spoke of *Weltliteratur* or the idea of world literature, by which he implied a living relationship between cultures not bound by dominance, provincialism or exclusivism (Jahanbegloo, 2007). Cultures are inherently dissimilar, Tagore believed, and not unlike Jung, disapproved of taking from others what was not one's own. Tagore invested in cultural explorations instead, through travels and correspondence, and endorsed a view of knowledge that was dialogical.[1] The anti-colonial, locally rooted universalism that he advocated was based on notions of difference and diversity, not conformity and compliance (Bose and Pande, 2011).

This book takes its form from the notion of *Weltliteratur* that Tagore referred to, using depth psychological ideas for understanding the intricacies of culture, with focus on the animus. The distinctions between Jung's concepts and Indian perspectives are many, and the notion of 'otherness' is therefore central to this work. That aside, Jung's concepts of anima and animus revolve around perceptions of gender in culture. I have drawn on the theoretical work of Jungians and used narratives and cultural perspectives from India and elsewhere, to bring psyche and culture into dialogue. The individual, as part of a collective, experiences tensions within it, and responds to these in particular ways. Notions of masculine and feminine are an inherent part of these intrapsychic and interpsychic dynamics, and while gender perceptions are not as binarized today as Jung envisaged them to be, contra-sexual dynamics of the psyche continue to manifest in varying nuances in contemporary life.[2] This book explores some of those unconscious dynamics in the lived experience of the individual in culture.

Some key themes in this chapter orient readers towards a discussion on the animus – Jung's experience of India and the place of culture in psyche, archetypes of culture, and narratives as a way of exploring otherness. The theme of cultural other is important, as the use of Jungian concepts in ideating about India implies that distinct traditions of thought are being linked. I wrote Jung's history with India in 2013, largely from the peripheries of the Jungian field. This work crystalized after I moved into the discursive realm of Jungian studies, experienced analysis in a cross-cultural setting and deliberated on the intricacies of Jung's ideas with fellow Jungians. It comes after a circumambulation, *parikrama* as one would call it, or a journey into the world and a return to origins. That place of return is made up of mutuality and difference, divergent and shared values, in diverse theoretical frameworks.

Encountering the Other

Jung's links with India and his journey of 1937–1938 were vital in affirming the notion of 'cultural other' (Sengupta, 2020, pp. 88–108). There were aspects of that journey that were illuminative for him, despite their alienness (study of the *yogasutras* and the notion of evil in Hinduism, for example), and those that evoked in him intense affect and bewilderment (his visit to the Kali temples, for instance). Jungian analyst Mark Saban describes 'otherness' as integral to the notion of Self, because the strange and enigmatic other affirms the 'the Other-within' the individual, a dynamic that was in Jung's two personalities as well (Saban, 2011, 2019). Saban explains how Jung's notion of Self is not a reconciled, undivided entity of transcendent unity, but a dialectical tension between sameness and strangeness. He reiterates Jean Laplanche's view that the tendency to domesticate the other, integrate or reconcile it with parts of the psyche that are familiar, is a totalizing move that erases the uniqueness and difference of the other.

Jung experienced 'the other' distinctly in his journey to India in 1938. The concept of *psychological* unconscious that he advocated was disputed by Indian philosophers whom he met and conferred with (Sengupta, 2013, 2020). The links between Indian academia and Freud, and the atmosphere of scientific materialism at the Indian science congress, were unsettling for him. Jung had undertaken an intensive tour of India for three weeks with a large scientific delegation before the onset of the congress, surveying prominent historical sites. The atmosphere in that gathering was intense, with dominant scientific personages from the west, encountering ancient Indian relics, in a colonial setting (Sengupta, 2013, pp. 99–180). Jung was indisposed after the tour, and his companion Fowler McCormick noted that he had a series of dreams after his visit to Kali temples, where he found the color red emphasized. Jung experienced the alien other in culture but did not think that the destructive aspects of these temples were altogether negative (Sengupta, 2013, p. 141).

Following his recovery, Jung reminisced with Indian philosopher Indra Sen about Freud, but the conversation became emotionally charged (Sengupta, 2013, pp. 299–302). The interview with Sen took place after the conclusion of the psychology session, where a paper by Ernest Jones had been presented. Jones' presence in Calcutta is not recorded in the science congress itinerary, although his lecture is part of published congressional records. It is likely that Jones' lecture was read out. The subject of Jung and Freud's relations dominated the congressional environment, prompting Indra Sen to ask Jung about Freud. Jones' indirect presence at the congress, a relatively unknown historical fact, can be understood today, given his close links with the Indian Psychoanalytic Society. R. Andrew Paskauskas' account of Freud and Jung's rift in 1913 highlights Jones' role in the political developments of that period and the formation of the Secret Committee (Paskauskas, 1988). Jones' paper at the psychology session of the congress referred to Freud's contributions, and was preceded by discussions among members about Jung's absence at the session. Jones advocated a distancing between psychoanalysis and other schools, with a statement that ideas expounded in other schools had already been incorporated in Freud's work (Sengupta, 2013, pp. 150–152). Jung experienced the other in Freud's indirect but distinct presence at the congress.

Jung's feelings of discomfort were also triggered by the scientific temper at the congress.[3] Jung's concept of the unconscious involved subjective and phenomenal realms, in approaches that differed from materialistic science (Cambray, 2011; Shamdasani, 2012; Jones, 2014). This was also the underlying reason for his differences with Freud (Falzeder, 2012; Shamdasani, 2012). Jung emphasized that his scientific approach went beyond materialistic and physiological assumptions. Science does not take into account the subjective and the personal, he argued, and psyche does not end where physiology ends. Besides, any objective inquiry of events is influenced by subjective conditioning; he called this the personal equation. The personal, subjective factor was central in Jung's work – psychology, in essence, was a personal confession (Shamdasani, 2003; Saban, 2014). Jung's ambivalence about rationalist science was re-invoked at the Indian congress. The concept of collective unconscious that he presented at the post-congressional events was distinct from the notion of unconscious that was deliberated at the psychology session of the congress. Jung's lecture referred to a universal layer of psyche, archetypes and transcultural symbols. A report of the talk, published in the following day's newspaper in Calcutta described the contents of the lecture, and referred to the mandala images that Jung used to elucidate his ideas (Sengupta, 2013, pp. 122–126).[4]

Despite his feelings of disorientation at the congress, Jung had several affirmative experiences during his journey. He experienced affinitive feelings at Buddhist shrines in Bodh Gaya and Ceylon (Sri Lanka). He studied the iconography of Hindu temples in south India and the architecture of Islamic mosques and forts in the north, and interviewed a Buddhist Lama in Darjeeling (Sengupta, 2013). He witnessed an ancient Kathakali dance performance on the Indian epic Ramayana in the southern state of Kerala, and enjoyed meeting friends and well-wishers. He interacted with priests, monks, philosophers, linguists, scientists, psychologists and educators during his stay, and had searching conversations with some of them. Visiting cards at the Jung archives in ETH and Jung's own personal diary entries confirm this. We know today that Jung went beyond established psychoanalytic conventions in engaging with eastern philosophical ideas. Unusually also, he refrained from imposing his ideas on India. He expressed his ambivalent feelings about the journey, and remained critical of the spiritual excesses of holy men. But eastern thought remained important, and he sustained his links with India till the end of his life.[5]

This recapitulation of events, and the feelings of affinity and otherness that Jung experienced in India, shows how distinct Jung was from Freud. The latter's distancing from culture and religion and single-minded transmission of psychoanalytic theories (repression and incest), based on a universality principle, governed his attitude towards alien cultures like India (Hartnack, 1990, 2001, 2008; Akhtar and Tummala-Narra, 2008). Psychoanalytic scholar Christiane Hartnack, who has traced the history of Freudian psychoanalysis in India, describes that cultural differences were discounted by Freudians in the colonial era, and pioneering Indian psychologist Girindrashekhar Bose, experienced this in the international psychoanalytic fold (Hartnack, 1990).

Girindrashekhar Bose was the founder of the Indian Psychoanalytic Society, and had met Jung at the 1938 congress in Calcutta; the two had also corresponded ahead of Jung's Indian tour. They had conferred about Jung's proposed lecture at the psychology session of the congress.[6] As the founder of the Indian association, Bose had his links with Ernest Jones. He was the first Indian to train in psychology in India, during the colonial era (Nandy, 2004). In 1922, he presented his concept of 'opposite wishes' to Freud, in response to the latter's theory of repression. Bose and Freud were not previously acquainted. Bose's doctoral thesis at the University of Calcutta in 1921 was titled *The Concept of Repression* (Akhtar and Tummala-Narra, 2008). Bose initiated correspondence with Freud about his research and the two remained in correspondence for several years, but never met. As founder of the Indian Psychoanalytic Society, Bose was invited by Ernest Jones in 1922 to be a member of the International Psychoanalytic Association. Bose's work of the early 1900s is the first known scientific writing on psychology in modern India. It was inspired by Freud, but was also independently developed, and established the foundation of academic psychology in colonial India. Bose suggested to Freud that the concept of dual wishes was not necessarily biological in origin. He had also found traces of latent femininity in the unconscious male psyche, and this was distinct from Freud's notion of a phallic ego (Akhtar and Tummala-Narra, 2008).

Bose proposed an underlying unity of the self in his concept of opposite wishes (Hartnack, 2008). Hartnack writes that Bose highlighted cultural factors in his research, but his views were not accommodated in the International Psychoanalytic Association. Conversely, Hartnack notes that Freud's ideas, too, were not easily absorbed in India. 'While central psycho-analytical techniques like the method of free association and dream analysis were applied in British India, it will be shown that psychoanalysis as a ther-apeutic method and as a cultural theory was not easily received in a culture with philosophical and scientific traditions, religious beliefs, myths, and cul-tural mores quite distinct from those of Central Europe' (Hartnack, 1990, p. 921). An asymmetrical relation existed between the two sides, and the tendency of the international group was to marginalize the 'other', or colonize it. Indian-American psychoanalyst Salman Akhtar notes that the Freudian group was more interested in the theoretical conquest of India, rather than questions of mental life (Akhtar and Tummala-Narra, 2008, p. 8).[7]

Jung's links with India, on the other hand, were based on cultural factors, since his encounter with Indian religious principles had intimated him about the notion of a unifying self. In the Tavistock Lectures of 1935, Jung said that although there was an extraordinary amount of unconscious in our civiliza-tion, the eastern world was conscious of things that the western psychoanalyst was barely aware of (Jung, 1955, para. 91). Jung's knowledge of eastern philosophy was gathered from Sanskrit texts and translations, accessed in Europe. I have traced these details in *Jung in India*. His journey to the sub-continent offered him an Archimedean standpoint, or a place outside the European world, from where he could view his work. He mentioned in his lectures that he withdrew from this world to travel outside, since his cultural sphere did not supply him with an Archimedean point (Jung, 2018, p. 1). Consequently, Jung's experiences, as much as they gave him an alternate worldview, located for us the place of culture in examining the unconscious.

Jung did not assimilate the full nuances of his experiences, and often found the contrasts between his ideas and Indian philosophy overwhelming. But, despite this ambivalence, he remained in dialogue with 'the other'. In 'Preface to an Indian Journal of Psychotherapy' in 1956, written for Samiran Bannerji a few years before his death, Jung noted that India's highly differentiated spiritual culture was distinct from Europe's, as the latter's origins were in Greek culture, and in sensory aspects of external world. He said that what was expected from India's spiritual attitude was an introspective viewpoint that would compensate the one-sidedness of the European outlook (Jung, 1955, para.1790). While spirituality may or may not be an overarching Indian trait, any one-sidedness, whether material or spiritual, necessitates working with the other. Jung un-derscored this, but was at the same time, skeptical about cultural explorations undertaken by westerners in the east, and the impact these had on the western mind (Sengupta, 2013, pp. 30–31 and p. 264).

Bridging Psyche and Culture

In 'Concept of Culture', American anthropologist Leslie A. White wrote that culture is a disputatious idea, and there is discordance between its material and abstract aspects (White, 1959). White argued that for some, material objects (art, tools, structures, events) constitute culture, while for others, culture is an abstraction. He believed that the Tylorian (Edward B. Tylor) concept of culture as a 'complex whole' that incorporates knowledge, art, habits and abilities *does not* bring out the difference between culture and human behavior. The intangible, imperceptible quality of culture, and its expression in human behavior, takes it into the realm of psychology, and blurs the ontological status of culture studies. White argued that somatic and subjective responses to objects and events in culture are distinct from the relationship between objects themselves in an extrasomatic context, and that the latter pertains to anthropology and culturology, while the former, to human psychology. It is precisely the emotions, sensations, affect, images and fantasies that are induced in our being in relation to people, events and objects around us, that are explored here about the psyche and the animus. The context is crucial, White says, for differences in context evoke different feelings, associations and fantasies. The symbol of the cow, for instance, has distinct cultural connotations in a Hindu religious world, when compared to Islamic or Christian societies, and will produce different emotional associations in the unconscious.

Jungian psychoanalyst Michael Vannoy Adams explains that while the Freudian approach reduced cultural aspects to biological and personal, Jung tended to relegate all psychic contents to the collective unconscious and archetypal. Although Joseph Henderson identified a separate layer of the psyche as the cultural unconscious, Adams thinks that the under-representation of cultural aspects in Jungian psychology, and conflation of archetypal with cultural, prevents genuine multicultural psychoanalysis from emerging (Adams, 1996).

The significance of cultural factors for the unconscious is clearer when we look at the notion of archetypes. Jung's notion of archetypes has been critiqued in depth, and I will offer a bare outline of the concept here, as it is integral to our discussion on the animus. What White construes as objects or events that evoke subjective human responses, are symbols that have collective significance and evoke affective responses in our being. Jung argued that the unconscious psyche was not made of repressed instincts or personal complexes alone, but had an archaic substrate, with universal resonance. The structuring patterns of the unconscious reflect primordial types, similar to Plato's Ideal Forms or Levy-Bruhl's 'representations collectives' (Jung, 1969a, paras. 5 & 6). The collective unconscious contains psychic life of our ancestors, from its very beginning (Jung, 1969c, para. 230). Jung named these universal structural symbols 'archetypes'. In *Archetypes and the Collective Unconscious*, he described how the gradual loss of relationship with symbols in Protestant Christianity induced an alienation from myths and a yearning for all that had been cast away from the conscious world (Jung, 1969b, pp. 3–41). Archetypes act as bridges with these worlds and convey shared meanings about human existence - for instance, notions of father, mother, child, God, hero, birth, death, initiation - common to all cultures.

Jung's emphasis about the archetype was in its archaic and universal character, since the psyche has an ancestry that goes back a million years, he said. (Jung, 1967, p. xxiv). He insisted that archetypes were empirical phenomena of the psyche, and not metaphysical or philosophical ideas. Their essence could not be reduced to biological instincts, although instincts were part of archetypes. The archetypal image could be described as the instinct's perception of itself (Jung, 1969c, para. 277). Universality of archetypes did not imply identicalness or fixed meaning. Jung noted that any attempt to derive one-sided meaning about the archetype, the symbol or image is futile, as it is essentially a complex entity. Archetypes reveal psychic opposites and the irreconcilability of opposites, and although they are not conscious entities, consciousness itself rises from them (Jung, 1969c, para. 407).

Jung's description of archetypes as archaic structures and primordial symbols alienated his concepts from established psychoanalytic theories. Unconscious phenomena could be found expressed in individual complexes, affect, dreams, visions, synchronicities; their universal occurrence meant a universal basis of the psyche. Jungian analyst Paul Brutsche, in his book *Creativity*, shows how images reveal unconscious psychic life (Brutsche, 2018). Brutsche elaborates on this inner subjective world through a series of paintings and comes up with astonishing observations about the psychological life represented in these images. The image is a repository of information about the unconscious, and its mysterious pathways between light and dark, Brutsche tells us. The image and symbol have been in culture from prehistoric times, before scientific inquiries about the unconscious emerged. We will consider links between archetype and image more specifically in examples later on.

Jung's concept of the archetype has produced numerous debates in post-Jungian discourse. Jungian analyst Warren Colman says that while most of Jung's theory of archetypes may be disprovable, the aspect of numinosity is not (Colman, 2018). In Colman's view, archetypes, as essentially unknowable and indefinable symbols, imbued with a priori and eternal meanings, render them vague. He suggests that archetypes as emergent forms of meaning that are shaped by embodied activity and affective engagement with the world is a more convincing description of the concept (Colman, 2018).

Jungian analyst George Hogenson says that the innateness of archetypes, explained through neo-evolutionary models of inherited genetic structures, is simplistic. Referring to Jung's influence from Henri Bergson and examples of animal behavior that show evolutionary consciousness, archetypes may be understood as instinctual tendencies of thought and behavior in all organic beings that are active in a collective context (Hogenson, 2019). Hogenson's notion of archetypes as shaped by environment affirms that culture is critical in understanding the nuances of the archetype. Christian Roesler asks if archetypes are transmitted through culture or biology. Arguing that the innate, instinctual and universal elements of complex archetypes have not been conclusively established in Jungian discourse, Roesler says that inter-generational, cultural transmission of ideas could explain the shared meanings found in archetypes. Roesler draws attention to the fact that the term 'archetype' existed in 1900s, and that Jung's Word Association Tests, study of complexes and encounter of mythic motifs in his patients' dreams intimated him about its psychological value. Meanings about archetypes, archetypal images or archetypal structures are not obtained from genetic or inherited sources, but emerge through environmental and cultural interactions (Roesler, 2012).

Clinical psychologist and Jungian scholar Roger Brooke offers a phenomenological view of archetypes. Brooke states that Jung's use of the term *imago* in 1912 for psychological complexes anticipated the notion of archetype as typical formations, or trans-individual, racial memories of the psyche, that have obvious analogies to myths. In his essay *On the Nature of the Psyche,* Jung distinguished archetypes from archetypal representations. Brooke writes that Jung defined archetypes as psychoid factors without content, or irrepresentable basic forms that have no consciousness of their own. Jung's mystification of the notion of archetypes as inherited unconscious images instead of structural forms, and his comparison of archetypes with Plato's forms, Kant's categories and Schopenhauer's prototypes, have not been very helpful, Brooke thinks. Archetypes manifest in bodily behaviour, in images and in affective states, much like the complex. They also constellate in primal situations like birth, death, marriage and motherhood, and during significant life-transitions. However, Jung consistently failing to provide a theoretical basis for the cultural-historical dimensions of archetypes has been disadvantageous, according to Brooke. He thinks that the archetype as a being-in-the-world expression of incarnate reality that includes the body in relation to culture and history, offers a hermeneutic and phenomenological basis for the concept (Brooke, 2015).

The debates around archetypes and emergence theory have been crucial in the development of the concept, but these discussions have not consulted adequately perhaps, examples from India, where symbols have been a predominant part of culture from an ancient time. In building dialogical bridges between Jungian concepts and Indian thought, the unifying notion of archetypes is helpful. While it is not the aim here to delve into all aspects of the debates on archetypes, for the purpose of our discussion, it is useful to consider, perhaps, the question of a priori and universal meaning, and the differences and contrasts that archetypes reveal when placed in specific cultural contexts.

Some Examples

Some examples from 500 BCE to sixth century CE, India are cited here in discussing the primordiality of archetypes. The figure of a 'dancing girl' (2300–1750 BCE) from Indus Valley (Mohenjodaro) Civilization is an archetypal image of the feminine, that illustrates how meanings about feminine and masculine are generated in culture. The excavated sculpture (see Figure 1.1) shows a figure, crafted in bronze, bearing an enigmatic facial expression. It has been described as 'a female dancer' of the Indus Valley Civilization by early archaeologists. An inquiry into how female figures have been described in archaeological studies shows cultural and gender filters at play (Clark, 2003). Sharri R. Clark argues that gender binarizing or characterizing the feminine in certain ways, with qualities of eroticism and fertility, and the masculine with its reverse, may not have been an active practice in ancient societies. She notes that theoretical tensions about these issues have pushed scholars to agree that the early feminine figures of the Indus Valley are not all fertility symbols. Several of the figurines show male and female features blended, for instance, beards and conical breasts, and these have now been described as 'ambiguous figurine fragments'. Clark suggests that while the images may reveal fluid and non-binary notions of gender in early Harappa and Mojenjodaro civilizations, their characterization into rigid and stereotypical 'male' and 'female' representations is cultural construction of a later age. The dancing girl is an archetypal image whose meaning is formed in the environment in which it is viewed. In describing the figures, perceptions about masculine and feminine are found to be active. The images themselves may denote no fixed qualities of gender, but gender-specific meanings emerge in the collective in which they are viewed. The dancing girl sculpture depicts an ambivalent feminine symbol, identifiable as a woman, but without fixed characteristics or a priori attributes (Figure 1.1).

With respect to universality and pre-historicity of symbols, the Indian text *Natyashastra* (second century CE) shows human emotions grouped into nine dominant types. A contemporary study identifies human emotionality in similar ways, parallel to this ancient premise (Hejmadi, Davidson and Rozin, 2000). The aesthetic principles that evolve from the nine dominant emotional states or Navarasas are part of Indian dramaturgy and performing arts traditions.

FIGURE 1.1 Dancing Girl of Mohenjo-Daro

Source: Gary Lee Todd, CC0, via Wikimedia Commons, https://commons.wikimedia.org/wiki/File:Dancing_girl_of_Mohenjo-daro.jpg

Neuroscientist Jaak Panksepp's concept of 'affective consciousness' and classification of seven primary emotions correspond with the ancient Indian classification (Panksepp, 2011). American psychologist Paul Ekman's classification of basic or universal emotions, and the theory of social emotions developed in the 1990s, also correspond with the ancient Navarasas. The similarities between Panksepp's theory and Indian Navarasas, suggest an archetypal basis of knowledge, with universal consistencies. Though the theories are not identical, there are similarities and parallels. Jung referred to these recurrent similarities as emanating from a universal layer of the psyche.

Elsewhere, human evolution has been portrayed in theriomorphic and anthropomorphic forms in myths like the Dasavatara (avatars of Vishnu) (Macfie, 1993). They can be compared with Jung's mythic and allegorical elaborations of the psyche (Jung, 1967). While the contents of myths across cultures are not alike (for example, the flood myth in the *Puranas* and the Christian flood myth), mythic imagination and symbolic patterns of thought have existed across cultures, and have archaic origins. A primordial basis for archetypes may be discerned from these examples, although this does not mean that archetypes and archetypal images convey identical and fixed meanings because of their universal occurrence.

Cultural Other

In an essay titled 'Sarah, Sabina, Gradiva: Three Women Splendid in Walking', Jungian analyst Linda Carter describes the spirit of Gradiva, a mythological figure in an ancient Roman bas relief (Carter, 2020). A dramatized presentation of Sabina Spielrein's life in an *Art & Psyche* conference in 2019 inspired her thoughts about three women who have been splendid in walking. 'With straight posture, clarity of thought, directness of gaze, chin up, this is someone in full self-possession, honest and articulate, who strides across the stage with firm grace and style' (Carter, 2020, p. 432). Carter notes that Sarah Berry-Tschinkel's performance reflected this, in a woman's fierce will to navigate difficult life situations. It symbolized Sabina Spielrein's life, her difficult childhood, relations with Jung and her role in mediating tensions between Jung and Freud, and finally, her independence in seeking her own professional path. The figure Gradiva (inspired by the Roman god of war walking into battle, Mars Gradivus) first surfaced in a Viennese novel written by Wilhelm Jensen. The protagonist of the novel encounters a mysterious feminine figure in his dreams, that prompts him to pursue its source. The case was brought to Freud in 1908 and interpreted by him through instinctual theories, which, Carter argues, does not capture the essence of Gradiva.

The figure of (Figure 1.2) reflecting the spirit of women who have walked through adversities, finds surprising resonance in images of Gandhi, the Indian nationalist leader whose iconic marches symbolized a nation's difficult road to

FIGURE 1.2 Gradiva – She Who Walks

freedom. The political context of these images is distinct from the individual feminine figures that Carter portrays. Cultural historian Sumathi Ramaswamy interprets Gandhi's walks as symbolic of his creative politics, where the deliberate act of walking, staff in hand, signified Gandhi's fierce stance about independence from British domination (Ramaswamy, 2020). The conservative Gandhi, a bar-at-law, who practiced successfully in court, before he became the Mahatma, embraced a stark, austere life and public persona that emblemized his concept of self-rule and self-reliance. Ramaswamy writes, 'Gandhi is the only man among the great public figures and fathers of the nation of the long twentieth century to make such a public spectacle of his partly clad body … . In so doing, the Mahatma was undoubtedly practicing a form of sartorial disobedience against a Victorian cultural formation in which bare flesh was denigrated as savage and uncivilized, a sign of lack of respectability and virtue' (Ramaswamy, 2020, p. 38). Gandhi's semi-clad body and forceful gait, memorialized by scores of artists and photographers across the world, symbolized the germ of a political consciousness, that became foundational to freedom movements worldwide. Martin Luther King's March to Selma in 1965 is a close parallel. The Roman god of war Mars Gradivus, walking into battle, is an apt descriptor of Gandhi's image as he conducted the Dandi March (Figure 1.3).

The archetype, within its universal connotations, carries nuances that are specific to culture, which render it with vastly different meanings. The two images, within the singularity of the act of walking, are distinct in their representation—the fully robed figure of Gradiva, self-reflexive, with a firm gait, and the stark, earthy, contours of Gandhi's bare body, symbolizing radical political action. The latter evokes images of a turbulent political history, distinct from the individual journeys of women in Carter's essay. The universality of archetypes is complemented by their particularity and contrast. Gandhi's walks were enacted in a collective, as premeditated political acts, aimed at arousing political consciousness. They are distinct from the solo journeys of the three women, although both images represent the archetypal act of walking.

The differences in archetypes can be seen in myths as well. The Vedic myth of flood, in which Manu, the first man, is engulfed by a flood and then saved by a fish (an avatar of Vishnu), is distinct from flood myths found elsewhere. Myth theorist James Fraser (1854–1941) found striking similarities of flood myths across the world in Babylonian, Sumerian, Hebrew and biblical cultures. The elements of flood, ancestral man and boat are common to all of them (Fraser, 1916). Fraser gives an elaborate description of myths in each of these traditions, which, while having predominant structural similarities, contain differing motifs and contents. Fraser does not include the Hindu Vedic myth of flood in his essay, where the flood, the first man Manu, and the ark (boat) can be found (Figure 1.4).

FIGURE 1.3 Gandhi – Dandi March.

Source: Carol M. Highsmith, Public domain, via Wikimedia Commons, https://commons.wikimedia.org/wiki/File:Gandhi_statue,_Indian_Embassy,_Washington_D.C.,_12389a.jpg

The Indian myth is distinct in its nuance. The primary mythic motif of a fish that mediates Manu's journey during an epochal flood. The fish is an avatar of Vishnu, created by him to save Manu and facilitate the survival of humans. The tiny fish seeks Manu's protection from predators in the ocean and is cared for by him till he matures. In time, the fish informs

FIGURE 1.4 Matsya Avatar – Vedic Myth of the Flood.

Source: British Museum, CC BY-SA 2.0, via Wikimedia Commons, https://commons.
wikimedia.org/wiki/File:BritishMuseumMatsya.jpg

Manu about a cataclysmic flood that will occur, and asks him to build a boat to keep himself safe. When a flood approaches, Manu takes refuge in a boat and ties the boat to the fish's horn, which takes him to safety in remote mountains. In some versions, Manu is accompanied by seven sages, who initiate various sacrificial rites, for the creation of mankind (Macfie, 1993, pp. 52–57). As an avatar of Vishnu, the fish is theriomorphic in character and has cosmic abilities; its place in Hindu religious life is important. The archetypal fish is rooted in rituals of the land, particularly in eastern India, where it is found abundantly in rivers and oceans (Banerji, 2005). It is ingrained in folklore, art, food, marriage and fertility rites, and fosters imaginal links between earthly and spiritual realms. The cultural traditions in the region reiterate the centrality of the fish and its life-saving qualities, and this renders the Vedic flood myth as distinct from other myths of this genre. Pertinent to mention here that Jung wrote that the fish symbolizes a duality, between its cold, deathly and unpleasant appearance and its creative and life-enhancing capacities. Its dual nature, is as an object of hatred as well as veneration. (Jung, 1969a, para. 187).

In highlighting the essence of archetypes, differences in culture and environment are often minimized, leading to an emphasis on universality. Personal associations to dreams take on new meanings when cultural nuances are brought in. As Hogenson (2019), Roesler (2012) and others have pointed out, the role of the environment in understanding archetypes is critical. This is evident in music, whose origins in the Indian subcontinent are, again, ancient. Ananda Coomaraswamy writes that 'music has been a cultivated art in India for at least three thousand years. The chant is an essential element of Vedic ritual; and the references in later Vedic literature, the scriptures of Buddhism, and the Brahmanical epics show that it was already highly developed as a secular art in centuries preceding the beginning of the Christian era' (Coomaraswamy, 1917, pp. 163–172). The Indian musical notes are grouped variously as *ragas* or *raginis,* and are aligned with emotional states or *rasas*; in some schools their rendition is tied to the time of the day and to seasons, to evoke specific moods. The structuring principles of music in the subcontinent are distinct from those in the West, although both are conceived around the same seven notes. The pauses, deferrals and free movement of the notes create a musical grammar that is unique to the region. It evokes fluidity in tone and timbre, rather than fixed, mimetic interpretations. Coomaraswamy writes that particulars of scale, rhythm and metre emerge in the environment in which music is composed, and within the region itself has many variations. Indian literary writer Amit Chaudhuri discusses that the tonality, tempo, narrative character and mimetic quality of Western music is distinct from Indian musical styles in his work *Finding the Raga* (Chaudhuri, 2021). The notion of cultural otherness is integral to archetypes, in differences of history, environment and religion, rendering them with vastly differing meaning in the psyche.

Tensions of Race and Culture

In discussing associations about archetypal images and highlighting the cultural, the personal need not be diminished. The personal, as well as the archetypal, offer a creative tension – inquiries into the unconscious need to bring the dynamics of both, as Jungian analyst Fanny Brewster says in her essay 'Wheel of Fire' (Brewster, 2013). Brewster makes critical note of how Jung failed to hold the personal and cultural aspects in the archetypal in his analysis of fifteen African American dreamers at St. Elizabeth's Hospital, Washington D.C., in 1912. Shamdasani writes that Jung's clinical investigations of 'Negros' led him to conclude that archetypal images have no racial distinctions, but Brewster notes that Jung's experimental subjects were made invisible without their cultural details, with no reference made about their personal associations to their dreams (Shamdasani, 2012, Brewster, 2013). 'Culture shapes consciousness—and this and the awareness we develop as individuals, as members of a particular ethnic group, and as citizens of the broader collective are important factors in the formation of identity' (Brewster, 2013, p. 71).

In contrast to his American subjects, Jung was able to locate 'the other' in his experience of India. While he remained open to dialogue and engagement about it, he was skeptical about journeys across cultures, and thought of them as detrimental for the western psyche. In his memories of Richard Wilhelm (1873–1930), the German sinologist who translated the ancient Chinese book of oracles, *I Ching* (Jung, 1989, pp. 373–377), Jung related how he understood Wilhelm's problem, as he had faced a similar conflict in his own life. The life of Arthur Avalon (1865–1936), the British orientalist who translated *Sat Chakra Nirupana* (The Serpent Power) in 1919, has some resemblance to Wilhelm's life (Taylor, 2001; Sengupta, 2013). Jung's reservations may be understood when we see how far Avalon (John Woodroffe) traveled in assimilating alien cultural material in his study of Sanskrit. Woodroffe's creative experiments took a toll on him after he returned to England, where he encountered a series of personal losses and withdrew from public life. The passage between cultures is not easily accomplished, Jung argued, as it induced a reversal of forces, with the unconscious psyche rising in compensation, to balance the conscious attitude. Jung encountered this in his journey to India, when he became too involved with the Indian world. The journey gave him a detached point of view eventually, but he had to exert a fierce will in disentangling himself from his surroundings and retrieving his conscious standpoint (Jung, 1989, p. 282).

Jung's attitude about 'the other', especially in matters of race, took a negative turn when he failed to hold a creative tension with the other. He fell into one-sidedness, especially in his views about Jewish and African people, and this has been deliberated at length in the Jungian field and outside (Samuels, 1985, 1993; Dalal, 1988; Brewster, 2017, 2019; Lu, 2020). Andrew Samuels' work is pioneering on this subject. I have discussed how notions of race have almost no scientific veracity and are driven by cultural biases and collectively held assumptions about 'the other' (Sengupta, 2020). This is not altogether different from colonial prejudices that prevailed in Britain in early twentieth century. Jung's remarks about the racial character of people reveal the extent to which he identified with collective attitudes, despite his own warnings about the need to keep individual consciousness separate from collective thinking. Speculations about racial differences and inferior mental abilities of other cultures are indications of the dark recesses of the psyche he slipped into, at various points of his life.

The theme of racial and cultural prejudices is important for depth psychology today, as Jungian work spreads into non-Western territories. Owen Berkeley-Hill and Claude Danger Daley, prominent colonial British psychoanalysts and close associates of Ernest Jones, responsible for training second-generation Indian analysts, displayed astonishing racial biases during their tenure in India. Indian-American psychoanalyst Salman Akhtar traces these grim and shadowy histories in his essay 'Psychoanalysis in India' (Akhtar and Tummala-Narra, 2008).

Both Berkeley-Hill and Daly published articles in *Samiksa* and the *International Journal of Psycho-Analysis* portraying Indians as inferior and infantile. They even spoke of a need for the British to take the role of enlightened parents for the Indian people. Berkeley-Hill (1921) wrote a paper entitled 'The Anal-Erotic Factor in the Religion, Philosophy, and Character of the Hindus,' in which he used Jones's (1918) work on anal eroticism as a springboard for describing the modal Hindu character as given to greed and hoarding besides being 'insanely short tempered and vindictive' (p. 336). Hill stated: 'No one can deny that as a general rule the Hindus exhibit a disastrous propensity to quarrel, especially in the family circle, and to this trait is added, what is still worse, vindictiveness. Reference has already been made to the miserliness, meanness and pettiness of the Hindus, and as these traits are so well known there is no call to notice them further … The tendency to dictate and to tyrannise is such a notorious trait of all Oriental character that it is not surprising to find it a prominent feature of Hindu character' [p. 336]. Daly, who did not work with a single Indian patient, wrote, 'In the Hindu, we have a psychology that differs considerably from the European, its equivalent with us being found in pathological cases.'

(Akhtar and Tummala-Narra, 2008, p. 12)

Akhtar writes that racist countertransference, distortions of group and individual psychology and complete disregard for the socio-political realities of India, not to mention the lack of consciousness about racist attitudes of colonizers, are explicit in these comments. Such dark and brutal acts of vilifying the other need continued scrutiny and critique, a work that Samuels has done concertedly, (Samuels, 1997, 2007).

Jung's prejudices did not seem to have surfaced prominently in his personal and professional associations with his Jewish analysands (Kirsch, 2012). Tom Kirsch notes that many first-generation Jewish Jungians experienced healing, self-empowerment and personal growth while in analysis with Jung. Kirsch writes that in *The Red Book*, Jung dialogues with The Red Man, a soul mediator, and attempts to bridge his Christian viewpoint with the Jewish. This was enacted with his analysands, James Kirsch and Erich Neumann, and Neumann's letters to Jung during the decade of the thirties, describe their intellectual and ideological differences (Jung and Neumann, 2015). In contrast to actual cultural differences that he experienced in India, and articulated openly, thereby introducing creative tensions between perceived oppositions, Jung's claims about race were clouded by generalizations of a dubious nature. He revealed similar limitations in his views about the feminine.

That apart, Jung's cautious and often chastising remarks to individuals on the drawbacks of cultural explorations, the oft-cited phrase 'going black', for instance, reflects an anxiety about the other, that is again, baffling. Irrespective of the pitfalls that such journeys hold, they have been part of human culture from early on. From the Greek historian Megasthenes, to the early pilgrim travels in India of Buddhist monks Fa Hien and Hiuen Tsang, to Iranian scholar Al-Biruni Venetian explorer Marco Polo orientalist William Jones and American writer Mark Twain to many others who recorded ethnographic, geographic and cultural details about India during their travels into the subcontinent, the phenomenon of cultural exploration has been integral to evolution of human knowledge. Iranian scholar Al-Biruni (973–1048 CE), advocated a scientific view of history, and bemoaned the lack of chronological account of events in Hindu scholarship. During his sojourn, Al-Biruni compiled information about ancient Indian sciences, astronomy, zoology, mathematics, medicine, minerology, and wrote about the social and cultural history of eleventh-century India, one of the earliest extant records of medieval India (Khan, 1976). These accounts helped in mapping worlds and revealed how the other was being perceived. The emotional and physical hardships that the journeys produced were not minor, but the desire to experience the other overrode the difficulties. Against this background, Jung's anxieties about cultural explorations seem exaggerated, which reduces the potential of knowing the other or accessing knowledge about self, in experience of the other.

Cultural Immersions

Two culturally immersive journeys of Jewish women in India in 1960s reveal the paradoxical feelings of alienation and affinity in encounters of the other. Jael Silliman, author of *Jewish Portraits, Indian Frames*, traces her family history in colonial and post-colonial India in a contemporary cultural document (Silliman, 2022). Silliman's narrative echoes other Jewish-Indian histories, and the peculiar contents of some of those journeys (Ray, 1996). It reveals the sequestered life of an upper-class Jewish girl in Calcutta, whose Baghdadi Jewish family retained its religious and communal ties with Israel, while living a full-fledged civilian life in India.

The experience of 'dwelling in traveling', or a life in shifting homes in the midst of domestic tensions, was both difficult and liberating for a young Silliman. The affluence of her parents' home and the conservative religious habits of her family seemed to coexist seamlessly with the stark poverty of the city they lived in, and its eclectic cultural heritage. This strange, multi-faceted life of a domiciled Jewish girl in one of the oldest cities of India, is not merely an account of a unique cultural intercourse, but evidence of how cultures have always been in relation, sharing the pitfalls and riches of fraternizations. Silliman continues to retain her Jewish identity in her secular, cosmopolitan affiliations, recalling that the poverty she witnessed in Calcutta helped her find her professional calling in humanitarian work in America. But it was in her eventual return to the city of her childhood that the depth of her involvement with the city can be felt. Building on her multifaceted geographical roots and her unique cultural inheritance, Silliman has established a premier Jewish historical archive in Calcutta, one of the first of its kind in India (see https://jewishcalcutta.in).

Mythology scholar and acclaimed American Indologist Wendy Doniger's *An American Girl in India* (Doniger, 2022) is a nuanced, complex, ethnographic account of her sojourn in India, at age twenty (1963–64), to learn Sanskrit and Bengali and study ancient Vedic texts. A Jewish American from the affluent suburbs of Long Island, New York, Doniger's journey into the pristine university world of Visva-Bharati, Shantiniketan, Tagore's creation, was characterized by numerous challenges and ordeals. Doniger oscillated between the joys of learning Sanskrit and Bengali, the company of talented young friends, distresses of tropical weather, unreliable living conditions and the horrifying sights of Calcutta's poor and homeless. The contrasts between her own privileged background and the grim realities of a young nation struggling to keep itself afloat haunted her, especially images of homeless children tended lovingly by their parents in the grimy, contaminated streets of Calcutta.

Doniger's enduring humor about the quirky styles and manners of the dwellers of a new land animates her episodic narrative, originally a bunch of letters written to her parents during her stay in India. Though it has historical errors (for instance, Visva-Bharati was never conceived as a finishing school, nor functioned as one), Doniger's observations are rich and revelatory. She recounts how the incongruities and uncertainties of her everyday life in India complemented the exoticness of the Vedic gods and Puranic myths that she studied, mesmerizing and baffling her at the same time. The hardships of a new environment eroded her health gradually, but Shiva, the trinitarian God, became her prized discovery in this period, the opulent architecture of the temples she visited serving as lasting influences of her Indian immersion. Memories of spring and autumn evenings of Shantiniketan, where she spent several months of her youth, served as remnants of a magical and difficult time. Doniger returned to her country of origin to become one of its leading Indological scholars, never letting go her scholarly interests in Sanskrit or Shiva - the wild, and frenzied god of Vedic mythology induces chaos, and an ancient language, singular for its complex semantics and grammar. She could not assimilate India and its strangeness fully, nor did she let India assimilate her, through an overvaluation of the archaic. She created something else out of this peculiar interface – a theoretical illumination of Vedic myths, channeled into contemporary cultural studies in America. A complex terrain for a Jewish scholar, who has remained, since her first journey to India, steadfastly rooted in Indological scholarship.

Doniger's Indian immersion resonates in other Jewish journeys in India and continues to produce exemplary writings of translation on classical Indian literature. Contemporary American Sanskritists Robert Goldman, Sally Sutherland, Sheldon Pollock, Paula Richman and others have brought a body of ancient Indian literature into western discourse through their scholarship and rigor, living between cultures. It involves difficult journeys, demanding apprenticeships and life in alien worlds. Sheldon Pollock has recounted the intricacies of these personal and professional sojourns in his reminiscences of India (see https://im.rediff.com/news/2014/jul/09_iapoy_sheldon_pollock.pdf).

Paul Brutsche writes that creative consciousness has two antithetical poles, the archaic and the modern, and floats between the demands of both to allow something new to emerge, 'internalizing the past and allowing it to gain a new lease of life in contemporary gestalts' (Brutsche, 2018, p. 183). The immersive experiences of Doniger and Silliman, Pollock, Goldman and others, bridge worlds without erasing otherness, balancing cultural peculiarities with desire and attraction for the archaic. The paradoxical nature of Doniger's experience, and the myths she studied, is reflected in her deliberations on Shiva, the erotic and ascetic God of Hindu cosmogony. 'Paradox is the very heart of Saiva mythology', she writes, explaining that these contradictions are mediated by Shiva himself in transcendent ways and are not a conjunction of opposites that produce superficial and logical resolution. They are oppositions that are irreconcilable, fundamental to nature itself (Doniger, 1969, pp. 300–302).

Doniger's and Silliman's sojourns also reflect a feminine radicalness, resonant of Gradiva, symbolic of women who walk difficult paths to find their own creative standpoint. Discerning in their ability to perceive differences, they diminished little of the complexities of what they encountered, forming creative wholes out of irreconciled parts. This is distinct from the characterization of Jewish people that Jung made, about their inability to produce their own cultural forms because of their nomadic existence. It is the experience of multiple traditions, in fact, that generated fresh fantasies in these scholars, transforming alien knowledge into new inquiry. Conversely, immersive experiences that did not include actual travel, and yet yielded important outcomes, can be found in the work of German oriental scholar Max Mueller, who never traveled to India but translated a compendium of Sanskrit texts.

Of Narratives and Interpretations

I have used narratives of culture in this volume as a tool for inquiring about the animus. Susan Rowland writes about how literary writing, (which Jung thought conveyed the discursive nature of psychological truths), reflects psyche's plurality (Rowland, 2006). The psyche is not a rational, monolithic realm, she says, but a dialogical exploration of subjectivity that attempts to remedy modern, logos-centred thinking. Rowland thinks that Jung's animistic, trickster-like, mythologically nuanced writing reflects this ambivalence, where origin and closure are not prioritized. Rational science excludes the other, or the notion of psyche as dual, paradoxical and opposing – it leaves out the unknown, uncertain and the arbitrary. Rowland highlights that Jung adopted a performative style of writing that expressed the dynamic, irrational, dialectical quality of psychological phenomena. The vignettes, stories, poems, images, histories, myths that are used in this book show the paradoxical and unfolding nature of the animus. They bring together familiar concepts and unfamiliar worlds, and reveal the tensions between archetypal, personal, social and cultural. The inner world is reflected in the outer, and the two overlap. 'The inner world is an inner landscape of nature and cities, castles and even space travel above the planet. To journey into the psyche is to wander in space and time beyond the usual boundaries …' (Rowland, 2003).

The narratives are drawn from extant sources, written and oral, and are narrated, keeping in view a hermeneutic inquiry of the psyche. They contain historical and ethnographic details about people and communities, that are familiar to me, since I inhabit a space in that culture. The aspect of dialogic subjectivity, where the narrator uses subjective contents from outside, in dialoguing with oneself, can be discerned here. Christine Widmayer explains how narratives that are not one's own, when evoked, become a dialogical way of enacting the self, in forming and reforming, since the self is not a fixed identity or goal, but an ongoing process. (Widmayer, 2018) The dreams and memories included in the book, are integral to the insights I have gained about the animus in a personal world.

In an essay titled *Psychology and Literature*, Jung said that literary and aesthetic work grasps underlying psychological phenomenon, as the human psyche is the womb for all arts and sciences (Jung, 1966). Literary content needs to be examined, not to encroach on literary domains and replace literary theories, or claim one-sided psychological truths about human subjectivity, but to offer alternate ways of seeing. The literary critic's approach to a piece of art is distinct from a psychologist's view, and often what is of literary merit is not psychologically interesting or useful. One approach does not invalidate the other. Jung also noted that creative work could be either psychological or visionary. The former involves familiar psychological experiences which may be explained, while the latter evokes daemonic, unfamiliar, grotesque and obscure fantasies whose meaning is not always accessible. This volume brings images of the animus from both visionary and psychological realms, parts that can be explained, and parts where meanings can only be alluded.

Some of the narratives are mythic in form. Bronislaw Malinowski (1884–1942) noted that myths have a performative dimension in culture, and recounting them in the collective adds to meaning-making. He also noted that contexts were critical, as myths have meaning only within shared contexts, and that they cannot be explained or universalized without taking into account ethnographic variations (Strenski, 2016). While Malinowski marked a class of sacred stories of ancient world as myths that serve a specific function of pre-serving collective ethos, the stories in this volume are not recounted for that purpose. Malinowski argued that Freud's concepts were culturally provincial, since they failed to note ethnographic variations, and tended to universalize psychological phenomena. He agreed that beneath the obvious surface of human life, a distinct realm of human emotions existed with its own rationale, whose basis may be biological. The conflation of culture with biology has been debated in many places, but Malinowski's thoughts about ethnographic dif-ferences and the meaning-making function of myths are relevant for us. Contemporary Indian cultural psychologist Ashis Nandy notes that the lan-guage of myths, as a preferred mode of communication, for a significant proportion of threatened and victimized cultures worldwide, has a unique political status and significance (Nandy, 1995). The concept of the animus deliberated here, brings narrative pieces in a broad range of cultural and ethnographic diversity – there are multiple social groups represented in the notion of culture, and the focus is not Sanskrit or high-culture. We will delve into the theoretical underpinnings of the animus first, before exploring its cultural and psychological nuances.

Notes

1 Tagore traveled to thirty-four countries across four continents, in a span of twenty years, meeting scientists, poets, journalists, artists, educators and writers. He refused to travel to Canada and Australia after being invited because of the racist immigration policies in these countries prevalent then. See Bose and Pande (2011).
2 I have used the term gender to signify social, economic, political and cultural contexts of men's and women's lives across the world, impacted by discrimination. Masculine and feminine are used to describe dominant perceptions about gender in social and cultural contexts. Both masculine and feminine attributes may be adopted by both genders but in most contexts, they are split and separated, with discriminative values attached to each. Masculinist societies have men in dominant roles in public places, with economic and political power centered around them. Women in such collectives are primarily in domestic and private spaces, in subordinate and invisible roles, with lesser economic, social and political power and access to resources.
3 Jung recounted to E.A. Bennet, that he had visited the Himalayas near Mount Kanchenjunga in Darjeeling during his Indian tour. For Jung, the myth of the mountain was animated at sunrise, but he thought that its significance escaped the scientists, because rational science had no place for myths. Jung's feelings of alienation were heightened during his congressional tour.
4 Jung's indisposition prevented him from presenting his lectures during the congressional celebrations, but he had the opportunity to deliver two lectures at the university colleges of Calcutta during the post-congressional events. Jung also lectured in Kerala and Ceylon. His absence at the Psychology congress was compensated a few years later by Indra Sen, who in 1946, as President of the Indian Psychoanalytic Association, delivered its presidential address titled, 'The Urge for Wholeness'. Sen's talk had extensive references to Jung's works. Sen founded Integral Psychology at Aurobindo's ashram in Pondicherry, where he taught Jung's concepts for many years.
5 Jung's last known meeting with Indian visitors was on his seventy-fifth birthday in 1950, when he received members of Indian Psychotherapeutic Society at Küsnacht, Zurich. He corresponded with this society till 1956, when he wrote a preface for the *Indian Journal of Psychotherapy*. Jung's last correspondence with an Indian medical doctor was in 1961.
6 Records of a few letters between G. Bose and Jung, ahead of Jung's 1938 Indian tour can be seen at the Jung Archives, ETH, Zurich. Jung could not attend the Psychology session due to his illness.
7 In response to a gift of an ivory statuette of Vishnu, received from Bose on his seventy-fifth birthday, Freud wrote, 'As long as I can enjoy life it will recall to my mind the progress of psychoanalysis and the proud conquests1 it has made in foreign countries'.

References

Adams, M. A. (1996) *The Multicultural Imagination: "Race," Color and the Unconscious.* London: Routledge.

Akhtar, S. and Tummala-Narra, P. (2008) 'Psychoanalysis in India' in Akhtar, S. (ed.) *Freud along the Ganges: Psychoanalytic Reflections on the People and Culture of India.* New Delhi: Stanza, pp. 3–28.

Banerji, C. (2005) *Life and Food in Bengal*. New Delhi: Penguin Books.

Bose, S. and Pande, I. (2011) 'Tagorean Universalism and Cosmopolitanism', *India International Centre Quarterly*, 38(1), pp. 2–17.

Brewster, F. (2013) 'Wheel of Fire', *Jung Journal: Culture & Psyche*, 7(1), pp. 70–87.

Brewster, F. (2017) *African Americans and Jungian Psychology: Leaving the Shadows*. London and New York: Routledge.

Brewster, F. (2019) *The Racial Complex: A Jungian Perspective on Culture and Race*. London and New York: Routledge.

Brooke, R. (2015) *Jung and Phenomenology*. London: Routledge.

Brutsche, P. (2018) *Creativity: Patterns of Creative Imagination as Seen through Art*. New Orleans, LA: Spring Journal Books.

Cambray, J. (2011) 'Jung, Science and His Legacy', *International Journal of Jungian Studies*, 3(2), pp. 110–124.

Carter, L. (2020) 'Sarah, Sabina, Gradiva: Three Women "Splendid in Walking"', *Journal of Analytical Psychology*, 65(2), pp. 431–439.

Chaudhuri, A. (2021) *Finding the Raga: An Improvisation on Indian Music*. New York: New York Review Books.

Clark, S. R. (2003) 'Representing the Indus Body: Sex, Gender, Sexuality, and the Anthropomorphic Terracotta Figurines from Harappa', *Asian Perspectives*, 42(2), pp. 304–328.

Colman, W. (2018) 'Are Archetypes Essential?', *Journal of Analytical Psychology*, 63(3), pp. 336–346.

Coomaraswamy, A. (1917) 'Indian Music', *The Musical Quarterly*, 3(2), pp. 163–172.

Dalal, F. (1988) 'Jung: A Racist', *British Journal of Psychotherapy*, 4, pp. 263–279.

Doniger, W. (1969) 'Asceticism and Sexuality in the Mythology of Śiva. Part I', *History of Religions*, 8(4), pp. 300–337.

Doniger, W. (2022) *An American Girl in India: Letters and Recollections*. New Delhi: Speaking Tiger Books.

Falzeder, E. (2012) 'Freud and Jung, Freudians and Jungians', *Jung Journal: Culture and Psyche*, 6(3), pp. 24–43.

Fraser, J. G. (1916) 'Ancient Stories of a Great Flood', *The Journal of the Royal Anthropological Institute of Great Britain and Ireland*, 46, pp. 231–283.

Hartnack, C. (1990) 'Vishnu on Freud's Desk: Psychoanalysis in Colonial India', *Social Research*, 57(4), pp. 921–949.

Hartnack, C. (2001) *Psychoanalysis in Colonial India*. New Delhi: Oxford University Press.

Hartnack, C. (2008) 'Colonial Dominions and the Psychoanalytic Couch: Synergies of Freudian Theory with Bengali Hindu Thought and Practices in British India' in Anderson, W., Keller, R. C., and Jenson, D. (eds.), *Unconscious Dominions: Psychoanalysis, Colonial Trauma and Global Sovereignties*. Durham, NC: Duke University Press, 2008, pp. 97–112.

Hejmadi, A., Davidson, R. J., and Rozin, P. (2000) 'Exploring Hindu Indian Emotion Expressions: Evidence for Accurate Recognition by Americans and Indians', *Psychological Science*, 11(3), pp. 183–187.

Hogenson, G. (2019) 'The Controversy around the Concept of Archetypes', *Journal of Analytical Psychology*, 64(5), pp. 682–700.

Jahanbegloo, R. (2007) 'Tagore and the Idea of Civilization', *India International Centre Quarterly*, 34(1), pp. 64–73.

Jones, R. A. (ed.) (2014) *Jung and the Question of Science*. London: Routledge.

Jung, C. G. (2018) *History of Modern Psychology: Lectures Delivered at the ETH Zurich 1933–1934* in Shamdasani S. (ed.). Princeton, NJ: Princeton University Press, p. 1.

Jung, C. G. (1953). *Psychology and Alchemy, Vol. 12, The Collected Works of C. G. Jung.* Princeton, NJ: Princeton University Press.

Jung, C. G. (1955) *The Symbolic Life: Miscellaneous Writings, Vol. 18, The Collected Works of C. G. Jung.* Princeton, NJ: Princeton University Press.

Jung, C. G. (1966) *Two Essays in Analytical Psychology, Vol 7, The Collected Works of C. G. Jung.* Princeton, NJ: Princeton University Press.

Jung, C. G. (1967) *Symbols of Transformation, Vol. 5, The Collected Works of C. G. Jung.* Princeton, NJ: Princeton University Press.

Jung, C. G. (1969a) *Aion: Researches into the Phenomenology of the Self, Vol. 9, pt. 2, The Collected Works of C. G. Jung.* Princeton, NJ: Princeton University Press.

Jung, C. G. (1969b) *The Archetypes and the Collective Unconscious, Vol. 9, pt. 1, The Collected Works of C. G. Jung.* Princeton, NJ: Princeton University Press.

Jung, C. G. (1969c) *The Structure and Dynamics of the Psyche, Vol 8, The Collected Works of C. G. Jung.* Princeton, NJ: Princeton University Press.

Jung, C. G. (1966) *The Spirit in Man, Art, and Literature, Vol. 15, The Collected Works of C.G. Jung.* Princeton, NJ: Princeton University Press.

Jung, C. G. (1989) *Memories, Dreams, Recollections. Recorded and edited by Angela Jaffe.* New York: Vintage Books.

Jung, C. G. and Neumann, E. (2015) *Analytical Psychology in Exile: The Correspondence of C.G. Jung and Erich Neumann.* Princeton, Oxford: Princeton University Press.

Khan, M. S. (1976) 'Al-Bīrūnī and the Political History of India', *Oriens*, 25/26, pp. 86–115.

Kirsch, T. (2012) 'Jung and His Relationship to Judaism', *Jung Journal: Culture & Psyche*, 6(1), pp. 10–20.

Lu, K. (2020) 'Racial Hybridity: Jungian and Post-Jungian Perspectives', *International Journal of Jungian Studies*, 12, pp. 11–40.

Macfie, J. M. (1993) *Myths and Legends of India: An Introduction to the Study of Hinduism.* Kolkata: Rupa and Co.

Nandy, A. (1995) 'History's Forgotten Doubles', *History and Theory*, 34(2), pp. 44–66.

Nandy, A. (2004) 'The Savage Freud: The First Non-Western Psychoanalyst and the Politics of Secret Selves in Colonial India', in *Bonfire of Creeds: The Essential Ashis Nandy.* New Delhi: Oxford University Press, pp. 339–393.

Panksepp J. (2011) 'Cross-Species Affective Neuroscience Decoding of the Primal Affective Experiences of Humans and Related Animals'. *PLoS ONE*, 6(9): e21236.

Paskauskas, R. A. (1988) 'Freud's Break with Jung: The Crucial Role of Ernest Jones', *Free Associations*, 1(11), pp. 7–34.

Ramaswamy, S. (2020) *Gandhi in the Gallery: The Art of Disobedience.* New Delhi: Roli Books.

Ray, D. (1996) 'Jews in Indian History after Independence', *Proceedings of the Indian History Congress*, 57, pp. 568–574.

Roesler, C. (2012) 'Are Archetypes Transmitted More by Culture Than Biology? Questions Arising from Conceptualizations of the Archetype', *Journal of Analytical Psychology*, 57, pp. 223–246.

Rowland, S. (2003) 'Jung, Myth and Biography', *International Journal for Jungian Studies*, 49(1), pp. 22–39.

Rowland, S. (2006) 'Jung, the Trickster Writer, Or What Literary Research Can Do for the Clinician', *Journal of Analytical Psychology*, 51, pp. 285–299.

Saban, M. (2011) 'Entertaining the Stranger', *Journal of Analytical Psychology*, 56, pp. 92–108.

Saban, M. (2014) *Science Friction: Jung, Goethe and Scientific Objectivity in Jung and the Question of Science*. London: Routledge.

Saban, M. (2019) *'Two Souls Alas': Jung's Two Personalities and The Making of Analytical Psychology*. Asheville, NC: Chiron Publications.

Samuels, A. (1985) *Jung and the Post-Jungians*. London: Routledge & Keegan Paul.

Samuels, A. (1993) *The Political Psyche*. London: Routledge.

Samuels, A. (1997) 'Jung and Anti-Semitism'. *Institute of Historical Research, University of London*, https://sasspace.sas.ac.uk/4412/1/Jung_And_Antisemitism_by_Andrew_Samuels__Institute_of_Historical_Research.pdf.

Samuels, A. (2007) *Politics on the Couch. Citizenship and the Internal Life*. London: Routledge.

Sengupta, S. (2013) *Jung in India*. New Orleans, LA: Spring Journal Books.

Sengupta, S. (2020) 'Indeterminate States in Transcultural Histories: "Cultural Other" in Jung's India'. *International Journal of Jungian Studies*, 12, pp. 88–108.

Shamdasani, S. (2003) *Jung and the Making of Modern Psychology: The Dream of a Science*. Cambridge, UK: Cambridge University Press

Shamdasani, S. (2012) 'Introduction', in *Jung Contra Freud*. Princeton, NJ: Princeton University Press, pp. vii–xxi.

Silliman, J. (2022) *Jewish Portraits, Indian Frames: Women's Narratives from Diaspora of Hope*. Kolkata: Seagull Books.

Strenski, I. (ed.) (2016) 'Introduction: Malinowski and Myth' in *Malinowski and the Work of Myth*. Princeton, NJ: Princeton University Press, pp. xi–xxxii.

Tagore, R. (2019) *Sadhana: The Realization of Life*. Chennai, India: Notion Press.

Taylor, K. (2001) *Sir John Woodroffe, Tantra and Bengal: 'An Indian Soul in a European Body'*. London: Routledge.

White, L. (1959) 'The Concept of Culture', *American Anthropologist, New Series*, 61(2), pp. 227–251.

Widmayer, C. (2018) 'Dialogic Subjectivity: Narrating the Self in Stories about Others', *Narrative Culture*, 5(1), pp. 15–33.

2

THE ANIMUS

A Little Book

Nearly two decades ago, around the time I began analysis and joined a basic Jungian education program, I had a dream, whose meaning I could barely fathom. It had an image of a book, red in color, on which, written in capitals and in golden, was a solitary word – 'animus'. The image conveyed nothing in particular, as having begun Jungian education then, I was not familiar with the term, or with Jung's oeuvre. The contents of the book were not visible, but the letters on the cover were illuminated. Over the next few years, as I began researching Jung's history with India, accessing large tracts of archival material, I tried to make sense of the dream, especially the veiled contents behind the book's jacket, but made no headway. In retrospect, it seems the hidden contents of the book were revealed in the lived experience of those years. When I began contemplating the image again, some years later, a publishing editor got in touch, asking if I had a book proposal in mind.

Synchronistic phenomena have been linked to emergence and complexity theories, to chaos and self-organization, psychoid state, '*l'abaissement du niveau mental* and de-integrative and reintegrative processes of the psyche' (Main, 2004; Cambray, 2009; Hogenson, 2009). Roderick Main notes the centrality of the psychoid factor in Jung's notion of synchronicity, but Jungian analyst Rosemary Gordon thinks that de-romanticizing archetypal images is critical (Gordon, 1993).

Synchronistic events in initiatory journeys are not uncommon. Cross-cultural affiliations are likely places of their emergence, as Shen Heyong in his essay 'C.G. Jung and China: A Continued Dialogue' has illustrated (Heyong, 2009). Joe Cambray's reference to Ilya Prigogine's work on complexity theory,

DOI: 10.4324/9780429423727-2

or the emergence of order from chaos, highlights that synchronicities occur in individuating journeys, during critical life transitions. George Hogenson suggests that synchronicity aligns unconscious complex, symbol, self and archetype in interconnected ways. Cambray, notes occasional traumatic, chaotized psychic states and affective intensity in individuals, encountering synchronicity. The symbol or image is a unifying factor in such cases, and signifies an emergent psyche, but the image does not have a priori, fixed or universal meaning.

Roderick Main mentions that Jung did not specify if the inner and outer conditions of synchronicity are momentary or long-lived. The self-organizing processes of the psyche that synchronicities signify can be expected to be long-drawn; its intensity is reflected in the numinosity of the image and its accompanying affect. I locate Jung's idea of the numinous in an intermediate realm of psyche and spirit, wherein affective feelings about synchronistic events and associations to the transpersonal, if any, are accompanied by analytic thinking and self-reflexivity. The little book appeared like a connector between two worlds – an alien psychology and a subjective psyche, united through a single image.

In his chapter titled 'Anima and Animus' in *Two Essays on Analytical Psychology*, Carl Jung wrote about the contents of the psyche that are intimate to us but do not belong to us. The image he used for this was of a house, whose contents live with us and act on us, but are not us (Jung, 1966, para. 329). Jung went on to describe, not for the first time, how differentiation is the basis of consciousness, *sine qua non*. He proposed the term 'unconscious other' in describing contents of the psyche that are unknown and alien. This, he said, was fundamental to the structure of the psyche, as it is also to the concept of the animus.[1]

The image of a house, inhabited by others is not just Jung's. In a mystic Indian tradition of Bauls, a breakaway social group of wandering minstrels, a familiar song runs like this:

You do not know who lives in your house,
You do not know how many live in your house.
There is one who draws
And there is one who colors
Then comes one who spoils that art.
Who knows how many live in your house?

Baul philosophy is part of an esoteric spiritual tradition of mid-nineteenth century Bengal. It has elements of both Hindu and Islamic religions, but there are no historiographic records of its origin. Ethnographic and oral history studies of Baul culture reveal a body-centered spiritism, with an aversion to orthodox religion (Kuckertz, 1975; Hanssen, 2020). The cryptic reference in the song about 'the other' could be an allusion to the unconscious, but Bauls have no established tenets about the psychological unconscious, having evolved their music from religious traditions of the land, and from peasant and agrarian life in rural Bengal. Facts like this make it necessary for a cultural context to be established in viewing the phenomenon of the psyche, as lived worlds are intrinsically dissimilar and diverse across geographies. But first, a brief overview of the concept of the animus and its post-Jungian critiques.

The Problem of the Animus

Jung's notion of the animus as a contra-sexual opposite in the psyche was in many ways a pioneering thought. Jung had proposed psychic dualities as integral to the unconscious, and used this in his theory of personality types, in the notion of individual and collective, ego and self, conscious and unconscious, good and evil, two personalities and polarities of archetypes. To this, Jung added contra-sexual opposites of gender. Jung's concept of contra-sexual psyche locates a secondary, muted unconscious gender in the dominant gender identity of the individual – the anima for men and the animus for women. When contra-sexual elements are repressed in the unconscious, they take the form of autonomous complexes in the personality, break through conscious ego and erupt in irrational behavior. Jung's definition of anima and animus interiorized gender binaries and suggested dual and oppositional gender for all. These dualities are exteriorized in men and women, as masculine and feminine, and evoke various kinds of inner and outer oppositions in the individual. The segregation of gender indicates not just biological differences, but also socially and culturally constructed meanings about gender and their implicit inequities and biases. Jung's concept, it seemed, integrated this division by bringing them into the individual psyche, as opposites that could be related. It minimized biological and androcentric emphasis about the unconscious, and linked contra-sexual entities with soul and soul image in contrast to dominant theories of the psyche, that privileged sexuality and repression (Jung, 1971, para. 808).

Jung's formulation of the animus seemed different from the way the feminine had been regarded in the psychoanalytic field traditions till then. In 'Feminism, Gender and Psychoanalysis', Janet Sayers takes us through Freud's concept of neurosis and theories of phallic envy and their consequent rejection by feminists because of their acultural, ahistorical and misogynist assumptions (Sayers, 2016). Although subsequent writings of Karen Horney, Melanie Klein, Donald Winnicott, Julia Kristeva, Luce Irigaray, Juliet Mitchell, Nancy Chodorow and Judith Butler critiqued Freud's views, the body remained the key focus in psychoanalysis, through which neurosis and morbidity in women were explored. Patriarchy and sexual inequalities are also experienced through the body, it was argued, and notions of soul or soul image were not considered. Jung's approach to the unconscious did not privilege instincts and body over soul, but attempted to locate oppositions and dualities of the psyche, with individuation as a route for integrating these opposites. Contra-sexual archetypes act as a bridge between conscious and unconscious psyche, and offer a developmental path, transforming fixed and assigned gender concepts into more differentiated and nuanced notions of selfhood.

Jung's formulations were, however, not as straightforward as they appeared. The term 'animus' was found in Jung's writings on Miss Miller, in whose fantasies he detected a masculine Aztec Indian figure. Jung conceived this to be an inferior, undeveloped aspect of a woman's psyche, mentioning in the same essay the phenomenon of animus possession, by which he implied a disproportionate increase of intellectual capacities in women (Jung, 1967, para. 272). Subsequently, in describing the anima and animus, he took on culturally ascribed notions about feminine and masculine, qualifying contra-sexual archetypes with fixed and stereotypical attributes, such as Logos for men and Eros for women. He denoted the anima with irrational feeling, and the animus with irrational thinking. (Jung, 1970, para 80). He noted that anima and animus present deep-rooted problems for the psyche, with the problem of the animus being in women's false identification with masculine traits.

Jungian analyst Mary Ann Mattoon, while explaining Jung's contra-sexual concepts to be archetypal in essence, conceded that Jungians have often confused cultural stereotypes about gender with archetypes. The notion of the animus has been used pejoratively, to restrict women socio-culturally within a stereotypical feminine ideal (Mattoon, 1981). Others like June Singer have written about Jung's culturally determined ideas of feminine and masculine in conceptualizing the animus (Singer, 1976). In 'Mind and Earth', Jung wrote that the anima is the image of primordial woman composed of irrational feelings, and the animus, primordial man made of irrational thinking (Jung, 1970, para. 82). Taking collective perceptions of gender to be fixed and essential truths, and describing women's thinking as unconsidered judgments with no rational basis, Jung concluded that the animus problem in women triggered a disputatious nature in them (Jung, 1966). A woman possessed by an animus can only be reined in by a brutish male force, he commented (Jung, 1969, para 29).

Jung's descriptions adopted conventional gender notions in hypothesizing about the animus, and diminished how otherness could be experienced in the psyche, outside collective gender ascriptions. He ignored the complex social world where notions of feminine and masculine were being shaped continually. Jung privileged the archetypal, mythic, symbolic and a priori and also the patriarchal, in describing women and the animus, without considering the hidden biases in these gender constructs. The long and complex history of feminism has seen many waves in the last hundred years. Its expression in literature, science, philosophy, arts, politics and environment shows the evolution of feminist consciousness across eras (https://www.britannica.com/topic/feminism/The-fourth-wave-of-feminism). The social ground has been a vital sphere for understanding feminist ideology and praxis, especially in understanding how notions of masculinity and femininity are constructed. Jung's view of the animus omitted this realm, and the ways in which psyche was in interaction with the social, in shaping our imagination about the other. Jung took culturally ascribed notions of masculine and feminine as non-negotiable truths and was not concerned about their implicit biases. Social issues were not real concerns he said, but symptoms of the displacement of the real feminine (Jung, 1970, para. 243). The 'real feminine', it appears, was made up of fixed and predetermined traits about women, that had no links with lived histories.

Distancing himself from the historical context of women's lives, where women demonstrated thinking, agency, and creativity. Jung's descriptions about the animus focused on archetypal qualities of Eros in feminine, and their displacement in the unconscious with the activation of the animus. He remained concerned about overt masculinization of women, or the feminine psyche becoming identified with the masculine archetype. Following him, early analytical psychologists came to view the animus as largely morbid and negative, and sometimes exclusively so. In *The Interpretation of Fairy Tales*, Marie-Louise Von Franz wrote about the negative animus as a personification of death, that manifests in feminine aggressiveness, instinctuality, undifferentiated spirituality, feelings of isolation, lethargy and ambitiousness (Von Franz, 1970, pp. 168–197). In a chapter titled 'The Animus Problem in Modern Women', Barbara Hannah writes how women are incapable of having judicious opinions of their own, relying on collective judgments, making it necessary for them to turn inward, reflect and claim what is their own. She concludes that the greatest difficulty in modern gender relations is the inability of women to remain within their feminine instincts (Hannah, 2011). These descriptions show the contra-sexual animus to be of a problematic nature, with rational thinking and feminine instincts split, and the feminine psyche imbued with pseudo-masculine traits. Jung acceded to the creative potential of the animus, but only notionally. He stated that creativity is a man's prerogative, and that men should live as men, and women as women (Jung, 1970, para. 243). His remarks about feminine potential were overshadowed by anxieties about the irrational and obdurate animus, which he thought were signs of a falsely cultivated masculine persona in women (Jung, 1966, para. 336).

Jung also maintained that the unconscious masculine in a woman stood in opposition to her feminine persona and could raise problems with her adaptation in the social world, if it was exteriorized. The animus is an inner dynamic that does not have a function in the outer world (Jung, 1966, para. 336). It should be nurtured inwardly, with deference to the social world. Even though Jung started by defining contra-sexuality as critical for individual development, with its potential for bridging the unconscious and conscious psyche, he conflated gender stereotypes with contra-sexual archetypes in elaborating on the concept. Instead of bringing the polarities of the archetype into dialogue, its destructive and creative elements in relation with lived contexts, Jung characterized the animus as being problematic. Since the conscious feminine persona is dominated by the personal (family, marriage, children), the unconscious masculine in women is of an irrational nature, he said. Animus opinions are like unsubstantiated truisms, constellated in women because their conscious attitude is not rational.

Many early Jungians endorsed Jung's views about the negative animus, while conceding the presence of a helpful animus in a woman's psyche. They deliberated that distinguishing the animus from the shadow, bringing a more differentiated attitude to it, separating it from the aggressive and belittling animus, is helpful. Claire Douglas gives a useful summary of these early discussions and the history of the concept in her essay, 'The Animus: Old Women, Menopause and Feminist Theory' (Douglas, 1986).

Emma Jung and Toni Wolff were among the earliest scholars who shared their ideas about the animus and the feminine, based on Jung's concept.[2] Emma Jung traced stages of the development of the animus from power, word, deed and ideas to spiritual development, highlighting the negative disposition of animus voices. The inferior status given to feminine and the veneration of the masculine renders the anima and animus with distinct problems for men and women, she said. Unconscious identification with masculine is common, putting the woman at a risk of losing her feminine. Women's natural attributes are in domesticity, companionship and relationship-building, where feeling, intuition and sensation functions dominate rational thinking and Logos (E. Jung, 1985). If the animus figure is integrated in the woman, it should be in a subservient position and not against her feminine nature, she noted. These early characterizations of the animus render fixed attributes (of feeling and intuition) to women, essentialize feminine nature and cite domesticity and companionship as innate attributes of the feminine psyche.

Elaborating on the structural character of the inner feminine, Toni Wolff, separated psychological phenomena from cultural, sociological, historical and religious factors. She noted that the absence of a feminine image in Protestantism renders it with a missing feminine principle. Identifying four kinds of feminine forms, Mother, Medial woman, Amazon and Hetaira, she described their conscious and unconscious dimensions and related these to typology, collective unconscious and individuation, suggesting that all four feminine variants may be integrated gradually in the course of a woman's life. She rejected the idea that all women are biologically and psychologically structured to fulfill the role of mother (Wolff, 1956). In separating psyche from social and historical, Wolff's ideas interiorized psychic phenomena, alienating psychic life from the collective. Separation from culture induces a problematic split between the inner and outer worlds, a Cartesian duality, and also a delinking from gender perceptions and how they are shaped by culture.

Post-Jungian Critiques

Post-Jungian critiques have identified Jung's contra-sexual theory as flawed and essentialist. Claire Douglas cites patriarchal Swiss milieu and Jung's ambivalent feelings in childhood around his own mother (and her two personalities) as having contributed to his one-sided views about the feminine (Douglas, 2000). It is possible that Jung's work with patients and his collaborations with women helped him understand these dichotomies better, but Douglas notes that Jung's anxieties about the feminine influenced his theorizing about the animus. Jung separated the irrational, dark and erotic aspects of the feminine from the nurturing and inspirational. In the following chapters, we will see how these traits can often coexist in surfacing a complex and composite feminine self, in fluid and dynamic relation with the world.

Ann and Barry Ulanov have considered the archetypal feminine to be central in the unconscious psyche (Ulanov, 1994). Affirming the voice of the negative animus and its false bearings, they point at how the animus acts as a bridge to the unknown, the Self, which when obstructed, unlived or dissociated, makes the individual destructive and pessimistic. The animus has socio-cultural elements, they affirm. Demaris Wehr questions Jung's androcentric ideas and biases. The Ulanovs' view that women need to free themselves from patriarchal definitions imposed from outside is in contrast to Wehr, who says the inclusion of the patriarchal social context of women, sexism and internalized oppression is necessary to understand the feminine in the first stage of therapy (Wehr, 1987). She suggests that women's lived contexts and experiences in culture need to be integrated, to liberate the archetypes from their static and eternal meanings, since Jungian archetypes perpetuate a male worldview, eliminate women's identity and selfhood, and induce internalized oppression.

Polly Young-Eisendrath says that while gender is constructed culturally, and can foster any number of variables, it is still male control that is dominant in all major cultures and that social constructs play an important role inside the consulting room (Eisendrath, 1997, 2004). The animus as a contra-sexual complex may be completely split off, she says, if gender is dichotomized as solely masculine and feminine in men and women. As the dissociated projection-making factor of the personality, 'the other' carries idealized or devalued parts of ourselves that can constellate the animus as an unconscious complex. Eisendrath takes a constructivist approach in her therapeutic practice. She thinks archetypes are not a priori, but reveal themselves in specific cultural conditions and contexts, and the cultural factor is important in ascertaining what gender, femininity and contra-sexuality mean to individuals.

Naomi Goldenberg's critique of Jung's contra-sexual model of the psyche begins with what she believes is a false androgyny or integration of gender that Jung and the first-generation Jungians advocated (Goldenberg, 1976). Jung's sexist biases in denoting masculine-feminine as Logos and Eros, their in-built hierarchies, the notion of Eternal feminine and so-called absolute truths in archetypal images, the libido denoted as separate in men and women instead of it being equal in both, are problematic, she says. Goldenberg finds almost no merit in Jung's theorizing of gender, preferring Freud's line of a repudiation of femininity as the task of psychoanalysis. The slippery quality of Jung's concepts that insulates it from questioning, the notion of an unseen syzygy or contra-sexual whole in each individual, the assertion of a separate unconscious in men and women with little evidence of it, Jung's tentative theorizing of the animus as an opposite of the unconscious anima in men and the subjective selection of myths in endorsing the notion of eternal feminine are all questionable premises, says Goldenberg.

Verena Kast defends Jung's ideas of the animus (and anima), denoting them in both genders instead of privileging either. Explaining that Jung's biases were a product of his times, and noting that Jung wrote different things in different periods of his life, she sees the separation from parental complexes as primary in the realization of the positive aspects of the archetype. Archetypal experiences are determined by both inner relational patterns and external climate, and though she signifies culture, her focus is on the therapeutic setting in elaborating the contents of the archetype (Kast, 2006).

Warren Colman refers to Object Relations theory in explaining how he encounters the animus and anima in clinical settings (Colman, 1996). It includes the patient's desire or hatred towards parental objects as basis of fantasies about feminine and masculine. The missing Oedipal dimension and sexual aspects in the animus, make it a static rather than a dynamic concept, Colman feels. Rendering contra-sexuality to both genders, or denoting it in generic ways as 'the other', is not satisfactory. Sexual relationship, sexual identity and the resolution of the Oedipal conflict are crucial in the development of the animus, he thinks. He adds that Jung's notion of contra-sexuality adds to Freud's ideas of parental complexes, and if synthesized with Object Relations, could be an important contribution to the field.

Lyn Cowan questions the heterosexist model of Jung's notion of contra-sexuality and the complete absence of sexual imagination in Jung's description of the animus. Jung's reaction to Freud's reductionist views may have helped him conceive the feminine/masculine dyad in symbolic and transcendent ways. But Cowan thinks that without parallel experience in the body, literalizing gender and sexuality in arbitrary and normative ways, makes Jung's concepts one-sided and alienating. Jung's notion of animus lacks a celebration of the erotic and the body, and indicates a collective repression of sexual instincts, idealizing of woman's reproductive roles and motherhood, and privileging Eros and relationality over everything else. The notion of sexual imagination and sexual encounters of a third kind, that counters unconscious heterosexuality has no place in Jung's contra-sexual theory, she observes (Cowan, 2002).

Post-Jungians Andrew Samuels and Susan Rowland each suggest that the creative aspect of Jung's unconscious, despite its essentialism, stimulates new thinking on gender, politics, art and imagination. Samuels offers ideas of emergent masculinity, good-enough fathers, the need for subjectivity in political discourse, and privileging gender confusion over gender certainty in Jungian theory. He notes the absence of discussions about other sexualities and suggests an approach of difference and otherness, rather than notions of innateness. One of the earliest Jungians who emphasized the influence of political and socio-economic realities on the 'private, secret, sacred, mysterious' story of gender, Samuels says that the division between inner and outer worlds is disputable, if not invalid (Samuels, 1985, 2001).

Rowland suggests that Jung's concept of the unconscious is filled with creative possibilities, allowing meaning to birth itself in new ways, deconstructing his ideas endlessly, challenging logocentrism and making his ideas fluid and trans-disciplinary in a post-modern context (Rowland, 2002). Jung's oppositional pairs in individuation make way for his contra-sexual gender notions to be constantly reshaped and rearticulated. Mark Saban hypothesizes this opposition in Jung's two personalities, fundamental to his conception of the unconscious, with Jung's privileging of the inner as problematic, as it encourages an erasure of real women who made contributions to his life and work (Saban, 2019).

In his reviews of the Fay Lecture Series publications on gender and feminine, David Tacey notes that the Jungian discourse on gender has always been separate from the feminist discourse, running almost in an opposite direction to it (Tacey, 2010). While contemporary feminism and academic gender studies would reject anything like the notion of the Great Mother, which implicitly conveys notions of an older patriarchal social order, the Jungian discourse would use these archetypes and ask for a reclamation of the feminine in culture. It is unlikely that even the notion of a masculine other in a woman would be accepted by mainstream feminists, he says, as feminism has always taken an ideological stance to fight patriarchy and masculinity. The gap between social and psychological constructs and between Jungian analysts and feminists seems vast, according to Tacey, with little in Jungian literature that actually engages with the social realities of gender. Tacey adds, however, that not everything can be explained by social construction theories, especially the autonomous, irrational, daemonic aspects of the psyche, which cannot be reduced to rational explications. The task of depth psychology, then, is to bring social and cultural constructs and the unconscious psyche into a tension with each other to evolve an understanding of the feminine in today's world.

From Archetypal to Transdisciplinary

Psychosocial studies scholar and clinical psychologist Stephen Frosh suggests that trans-disciplinarity differentiates itself from multi-disciplinary and interdisciplinary approaches by introducing tensions in research (Frosh, 2013). Trans-disciplinarity does not have holistic goals; instead, it is deconstructive and disrupts conventional academic boundaries. It attempts to include 'the other' in research methods, taking subjects from outside mainstream academia. Trans-disciplinarity questions conventional disciplinary agreements, the rationale being that the complex nature of human problems necessitates utilization of multiple approaches. But this is not intended for a unified resolution of the problem, he says. Rather it is about recognizing the essential fragmentation of knowledge itself, and its contextual basis, where paradoxes and contradictions are inalienable to consciousness and the knowledge we generate.

The fluidity of disciplinary boundaries, and lack of holistic endings convey something essential about the contra-sexual psyche, between conscious and unconscious, dark and light, inner and outer. Trans-disciplinarity opens up possibilities of linking disparate realms and discrete entities in social, political and psychological worlds. Andrew Samuels denotes the shifting and indeterminate boundaries of gender as gender confusion and ambivalence rather than gender fluidity, but I think that the fluid and liminal nature of contra-sexuality, is an apt descriptor for the complex, unfolding psyche in multiple social worlds.

Two or three problematic aspects about Jung's conceptualization of the animus. First, Jung's separation of the psyche from historical realities of gender, and his adoption of culturally dominant values about feminine and masculine. Second, Jung's description of the animus and the feminine psyche in one-sided and fixed ways, without bringing its multiplicity and ambivalences into the discussion. This contradicts his view that archetypes have no fixed meaning. Third, his prioritizing of the archetypal approach. While this has been critiqued by many, very few studies have actually explored contra-sexual dynamics of the psyche with reference to culture and social. Some studies have attempted to bring gender and sexuality into discussion in contemporary social worlds, but these studies do not discuss unconscious contra-sexuality (Akhtar, 2005; Ellman, P., Basak, J., and Schlessinger-Kipp, 2021).

Goldenberg's view that psychoanalytic theory could do without a feminine construct alienates psychology from feminist history, which David Tacey notes, is how feminists have rejected psychoanalytic theories, because of their androcentric biases. The social, economic, political struggles experienced by women in all collectives, less or more, is made invisible in Goldenberg's approach. An erasure of the feminine in psyche implies a repudiation of feminist history, denial of gender prejudices, refutation of women's struggles worldwide. Goldenberg's stance isolates the psyche from lived realities of gender, which in most contexts is still asymmetrical and unequal. However, she rightly interrogates Jung's a priori assumptions about the feminine and asks for inclusion of the body in discussion on the unconscious.

Colman's view, of integrating sexuality and Object Relations, body and parental complexes in notions of contra-sexuality, offsets archetypal emphasis on the animus. In Jung's defense it may be said that, although he diminished sexuality, body, attachment relations and the influence of social in conceptualizing the animus, he attempted to integrate archaic, indigenous worldviews in his concepts, instead of viewing the unconscious in narrow, solipsistic ways. He remarked that the importance modern psychology gave to 'parental complex' mirrors the centrality primitive man gave to the dangerous power of ancestral spirits. (Jung, 1966, para. 293). Jung's emphasis on the archetypal makes his concepts static, according to Colman, but Jung's views offered possibilities of dialogue with other cultures in viewing the unconscious.

Tacey's impression that feminists are opposed to masculine metaphors, needs more debate. The notion that the masculine psyche is essentially destructive and anti-feminine, is problematic, and is a stereotyping of masculinity. Is agency, aggression, thinking, masculine or feminine attributes? While each of these is present in both genders, cultures ascribe men and women with specific traits and roles, – Jung was distanced from this dynamic context of the feminine.

Feminine Histories

The changing paradigms of women's lives, which Jung placed outside his psychological purview, were in fact well manifest in the environment he lived. 1900s Europe witnessed radical shifts in women's suffrage, education, science, arts, sexual and reproductive rights. A review of women scientists of post-Enlightenment era shows early pioneers, and their struggles in having their work accepted in scientific fraternities. Sue V. Rosser traces the long chain of scientific inventions made by women, and their painful marginalization in academia (Rosser, 1987). Literary and philosophical writings in Europe reveal women's complex and isolated lives, struggling to break free of narrow, restricted social norms.[3] Jung witnessed these tensions firsthand in his women analyzands. Maggie Anthony follows the lives of women Jung met, collaborated or analyzed, in his psychoanalytic career (Anthony, 2017).

In introduction to C.G. Jung's 1925 seminar on Analytical Psychology, William McGuire describes Cary Baynes' collaboration with Jung, in translating and editing some of his important works (McGuire, 2011). Baynes was a resourceful and efficient collaborator, taking on patient consultation even, occasionally. Jung's experience with Sabina Spielrein and Maria Moltzer was critical for developing his insights about transference and countertransference. Psychology Club and the first Jungian institute in Zurich were formed with support from Edith McCormick, Jolande Jacobi, Toni Wolff and Emma Jung (Kirsch, 2004). Marie Louis Von Franz and Barbara Hannah disseminated Jung's ideas, as did Kristine Mann, Esther Harding, Jane Wheelwright and Hilda Kirsch. Mary Mellon set up Bollingen Foundation that helped publish Jung's writings, Olga Fröbe-Kapteyn organized Eranos conferences, while Christina Morgan and Kristine Mann helped Jung enunciate his ideas through their cryptic visions (Douglas, 1989, Jones, 2020). Many of these women traveled from far to be analyzed by Jung, in mid-1900s Europe, when women's lives were still largely domesticated and parochial. In all of them, and many other women whom he encountered in his travels (Ruth Bailey in Africa, and Alice Boner, Gertrude Sen, Maitreyi Devi in India),[4] Jung witnessed feminine vitality and thinking. This is not to undermine the importance of the dark and destructive elements of the unconscious psyche. But Jung did not always link the animating, creative qualities of the feminine with the dark and irrational, separating also, inner phenomenon from outer histories.

It is possible that Jung's proclivity for the archetypal and tendency to align every symbol, image or event with the unconscious psyche, made him less inclined towards historical realities, or personal particulars. His approach to Christina Morgan, whose hundred odd visions and unpublished notebooks, Jungian analyst and writer Claire Douglas has examined, suggests something similar (Douglas, 1989, 1997). Jung analyzed Morgan's visions, and used forty-four of these paintings in his Vision Seminars of 1930, explaining their significance, omitting personal details. Jung had introduced the process of active imagination to Morgan, after she began analysis with him. He found her initial output enchanting, and was captivated by the visionary quality of the images, but this view changed later. Jung's analysis, seemed to have helped her find the chthonic, earthly aspect of her femininity, but there were transference and countertransference feelings involved, that were not addressed. Jung became increasingly frustrated with her paintings, describing them as 'awfully uncertain, boring, treacherous'. He described Morgan's visionary process as not her own, but nature's wisdom speaking through her. Morgan struggled to find her voice under these conflicting currents, and in the final run, was unable to hold the separate threads of her life together. It seems that Jung's emphasis on the archetypal and the symbolic, resulted in one-sided views about the psyche. Ladson Hinton argues in his paper 'Jung, Time and Ethics' that Jung's privileging of the archetypal in contexts of historical and personal suffering led to a dulling of his ethical vision – Jung interpreted Nazi phenomena as an archetype of Wotan, or a cultural regression that would bring about cultural evolution in Germany (Hinton, 2019, p. 258).

Multiplicity of the Feminine, Weaving Inner and Outer

In *Exploring Depth Psychology and the Female Self*, feminist views gathered from somewhere, almost anywhere, the feminine is represented as amorphous, and fragmented (Gardner and Miller, 2020). The narratives embody feminine multiplicity, in contrasting and competing spaces, across diverse geographies. Here, feminine deliberations are not about attachment relations and early childhood experiences, but about the self in fragile, dystopian worlds. Authors break disciplinary boundaries between myth, history, politics, ecology, film and therapeutic practice, making space for the emergent. The contra-sexual psyche is ambivalent in this neoteric realm, as Frosh suggests trans-disciplinary approaches are likely to be, showing incompleteness of knowing, rather than fixed and inviolable truths.

Jung's principle of individuation encourages the individual to disengage from collective attitudes and look into oppositions within the psyche for evolution of the self. My contention is that interfaces between outer and inner reveal nuances about the animus that are more complex than the one-sided descriptions about the feminine that Jung came up with. The limitations in Jung's approach need not imply an inadequacy of the concept itself. A re-evaluation of Jung's views about animus implies a critique of his emphasis on the archetypal, his distancing from body, and from personal, social and historical realms and his problematic descriptions about feminine thinking.

Second, the collective is not a fixed entity with eternal, unchanged meanings, but a dynamic realm that is evolving continually. The individual's location in an environment and relation to it, influences the subjective psyche. The lived context of the psyche, tensions within it and cultural perceptions about gender makes the unconscious psyche a complex and heterogenous entity. Jung himself made forays into other cultures in order to understand the psyche in all its contrasts, paradoxes and divergences. However, he did not apply the same eclecticism in deliberating on the feminine and the animus.

From the standpoint of culture, Jung was able to hold his differences with India in his conversations and inquiries. The notion of psychological unconscious that he presented in his public lectures in India, contrasted sharply with the concept of unconscious presented by Indian psychologists at the psychology session of the congress. When asked about Freud, on more than one occasion, Jung's reaction was anger. His pleasure at being honored at the historic congress with a honoris causa was overshadowed by his illness, that prevented him from being present at the commemorative events. His enthusiasm in traveling to India, undertaking three thousand miles of journey within the subcontinent, was contrasted by his refusal to meet holy men, and the eruption of a major dream that directed his attention back to his European world (Sengupta, 2013).

In the dream in Calcutta, Jung saw that he was in front of the castle of the Holy Grail, on an unknown island off the English Coast (Jung, 1989). The illumined hall of the castle showed a celebration, but it seemed to Jung that no one in his group understood the essence of the Grail; the Grail was not a speculative concept for him, but a living myth. The dream of the Grail shook Jung out of his Indian preoccupations and returned him to his European roots, and to his own work. Implicit in this understanding was the notion of a cultural ground, one's own, fundamental to the work of the psyche. It is this cultural matrix in which the notion of the animus is deliberated on, in this volume. It implicates various dimensions of otherness; a falsely adopted masculine persona is not the only expression of the contra-sexual animus. The animus is a paradoxical entity, in dialectical tension with its parts, unfolding in complex ways, in the psyche.

Notes

1 Jung's writings on the animus can be found in the following works: 'The Syzygy: Anima and Animus' (in *Aion: Researches into the Phenomenology of the Self*, CW 9ii); 'Definitions' (in *Psychological Types*, CW 6); 'Anima and Animus' (in *Two Essays in Analytical Psychology*, CW 7); 'Woman in Europe' and 'Mind and Earth' (*Civilization in Transition*, CW 10); 'Marriage as a Psychological Relationship' (in *Development of Personality*, CW 17); and general remarks in other places.

2 Jung split Eros and Logos in women and men, conflating women with Eros and feeling, and Logos with men and thinking.

3 Virginia Wolff (1882–1941), an early feminist explorer, had written her important novels by 1940 and participated in the Bloomsbury movement. French existentialist philosopher Simone de Beauvoir (1908–1986) had written *The Second Sex* in 1946. Marie Curie (1867–1934) had begun her radioactive research by 1895 and faced discrimination in scientific academia. There were other historical instances in Jung's European environment, where women's independent thinking and rational attitudes were noticed.

4 Details of Jung's meeting with Ruth Bailey and their shared experience of Africa can be found in Blake Burleson, *Jung in Africa* (London and New York: Continuum International Publishing Group, 2005). Jung's encounters with Alice Boner, Gertrude Sen and Maitreyi Devi took place in India in 1937–1938. See Sengupta (2013).

References

Akhtar, S. (2005) *Freud along the Ganges: Psychoanalytic Reflections on the People and Culture of India*. New York: Other Press.

Anthony, M. (2017) *Salome's Embrace: The Jungian Women*. London: Routledge.

Cambray, J. (2009) *Synchronicity: Nature and Psyche in an Interconnected Universe*. College Station: Texas A&M University Press.

Colman, W. (1996) 'Aspects of Anima and Animus in Oedipal Development', *Journal of Analytical Psychology*, 41, pp. 37–57.

Cowan, L. (2002) *Tracking the White Rabbit: A Subversive View of Modern Culture*. Hove East Sussex and New York: Brunner-Routledge; Taylor & Francis.

Douglas, C. (1986) 'The Animus: Old Women, Menopause and Feminist Theory'. Review of *Women Growing Older: The Animus* by Jane Hollister Wheelwright; *Change of Life; A Psychological Study of Dreams and the Menopause* by Ann Mankowitz; *Feminist Archetypal Theory: Interdisciplinary Re-visions of Jungian Thought* by Estella Lauter, Carol Rupprecht', *The San Francisco Jung Institute Library Journal*, 6(3), pp. 1–20.

Douglas, C. (1989) 'Christiana Morgan's Visions Reconsidered: A Look Behind the Visions Seminars', *The San Francisco Jung Institute Library Journal*, 8(4), pp. 5–27.

Douglas, C. (ed.) (1997) *Visions – Notes of the Seminar Given in 1930–1934 by C. G. Jung*. 2 Vols. Bollingen Series XCIX. Princeton, NJ: Princeton University Press.

Douglas, C. (2000) *'The Woman in the Mirror': Analytical Psychology and the Feminine*. New York: IUniverse.com.

Eisendrath, P. Y.- (1997) 'Gender and Contrasexuality: Jung's Contributions and Beyond' in Eisendrath, P.Y.- and Dawson, T. (eds.), *The Cambridge Companion to Jung*. Cambridge: Cambridge University Press, pp. 223–229.

Eisendrath, P. Y.- (2004) *'Subject to Change': Jung, Gender and Subjectivity in Psychoanalysis*. London: Routledge.

Ellman, P., Basak, J., and Schlessinger-Kipp, G. (2021) *Psychoanalytic and Socio-Cultural Perspectives on Women in India: Violence, Safety and Survival*. London and New York: Routledge.

Frosh, S. (2013) 'Transdisciplinary Tensions and Psychosocial Studies', *Enquire*, 6(1), pp. 1–15.

Gardner, L. and Miller, C. (eds.) (2020) *Exploring Depth Psychology and the Female Self: Feminist Themes from Somewhere*. London: Routledge.

Goldenberg, N. (1976) 'A Feminist Critique of Jung', *Signs*, 2(2), pp. 443–449.

Gordon, R. (1993) *Bridges: Metaphor for Psychic Processes*. London: Karnac Books.

Hannah, B. (2011) *The Animus: The Spirit of Inner Truth in Women*. Wilmette, IL: Chiron Publications.

Hanssen, K. (2020) *Women, Religion and the Body in South Asia: Living with Bengali Bauls*. *Routledge South Asian Religion Series*. London: Routledge, UK.

Heyong, S. (2009) 'C.G. Jung and China: A Continued Dialogue', *Jung Journal*, 3(2), pp. 5–14.

Hinton, L. (2019) 'Jung, Time and Ethics' in Mills, J. (ed.), *Jung and Philosophy*. London: Routledge.

Hogenson, G. (2009) 'Synchronicity and Moments of Meeting', *Journal of Analytical Psychology*, 54, pp. 183–197.

Jones, R. (2020) 'The Snake in the Mandala: Dialogical Aspects of Jung's "A Study in the Process of Individuation"', *Journal of Analytical Psychology*, 65(2), pp. 385–407.

Jung, C. G. (1966) *Two Essays in Analytical Psychology*, Vol. 7, The Collected Works of C. G. Jung. 2nd ed. Princeton, NJ: Princeton University Press.

Jung, C. G. (1967) *Symbols of Transformation*, Vol. 5, The Collected Works of C. G. Jung. 2nd ed. Princeton, NJ: Princeton University Press.

Jung, C. G. (1969) *Aion, Researches into the Phenomenology of the Self*, Vol. 9, pt. 2, The Collected Works of C. G. Jung. Princeton, NJ: Princeton University Press.

Jung, C. G. (1970) *Civilization in Transition*, Vol. 10, The Collected Works of C. G. Jung. 2nd ed. Princeton, NJ: Princeton University Press.

Jung, C. G. (1971) *Psychological Types*, Vol. 6, The Collected Works of C. G. Jung. Princeton, NJ: Princeton University Press.

Jung, C. G. (1989) *Memories, Dreams, Recollections*. Recorded and edited by Angela Jaffe. New York: Vintage Books.

Jung, E. (1985). *Animus and Anima: Two Essays*. Dallas, TX: Spring Publications.

Kast, V. (2006) 'Anima/Animus' in Papadopoulos, R. K. (ed.), *The Handbook of Jungian Psychology: Theory, Practice and Applications*. London: Routledge, pp. 113–129.

Kirsch, T. (2004) 'History of Analytical Psychology' in Cambray, J. and Carter, L. (eds.), *Analytical Psychology: Contemporary Perspectives in Jungian Analysis*. London and New York: Routledge, 2004, pp. 5–31.

Kuckertz, J. (1975) 'Origin and Construction of the Melodies in Baul Songs of Bengal', *Yearbook of the International Folk Music Council*, 7, pp. 85–91.

Main, R. (2004) *The Rupture of Time: Synchronicity and Jung's Critique of Modern Western Culture*. London: Routledge.

Mattoon, M. A. (1981) *Jungian Psychology in Perspective*. New York: The Free Press.

McGuire, W. (ed.) (2011) *Introduction to Jungian Psychology: Notes of the Seminar on Analytical Psychology Given in 1925 by C. G. Jung* (Lectures delivered at ETH Zurich, Book 5), rev. ed. Princeton, NJ: Princeton University Press.

Rosser, S. (1987) 'Feminist Scholarship in the Sciences: Where Are We Now and When Can We Expect a Theoretical Breakthrough?', *Hypatia*, 2(3), pp. 5–17.

Rowland, S. (2002) *Jung: A Feminist Revision*. Cambridge, UK: Polity Press.

Saban, M. (2019) *'Two Souls Alas': Jung's Two Personalities and the Making of Analytical Psychology*. Asheville, NC: Chiron Publications.

Samuels, A. (1985) *Jung and the Post-Jungians*. London: Routledge, 1985.

Samuels, A. (2001) *'Politics on the Couch': Citizenship and the Internal Life*. London: Karnac Books.

Sayers, J. (2016) 'Feminism, Gender and Psychoanalysis' in Elliott, A. and Prager, J. (eds.), *The Routledge Handbook of Psychoanalysis in the Social Sciences and Humanities*, Routledge International Handbooks. London: Routledge, pp. 411–428.

Sengupta, S. (2013) *Jung in India*. New Orleans, LA: Spring Journal Books.

Singer, J. (1976) *Androgyny: Toward a New Theory of Sexuality*. Garden City, NY: Anchor Press.

Tacey, D. (2010) 'Fay Lectures Book Series: 20th Anniversary Reviews', *Journal of Analytical Psychology*, 55(2), pp. 300–312.

Ulanov, A. and Ulanov, B. (1994) *Transforming Sexuality: The Archetypal World of Anima and Animus*. Boston, MA: Shambala Publications.

Von Franz, M. L. (1970) *The Interpretation of Fairy Tales*, rev. ed. Boston, MA: Shambala Publications.

Wehr, D. S. (1987) *Jung and Feminism: Liberating Archetypes*. London: Routledge.

Wolff, T. (1956) *Structural Forms of the Feminine Psyche*. Translated by Watzlawik, P. Zurich: The Students Association, C.G. Jung Institute.

3

PHOOLAN

Bone and Marrow

In *Mysterium Coniunctionis*, Jung referred to the myth of the phoenix, its death and renewal. After burning itself, the phoenix revives from an unseemly worm, in a period of one day, before flying away to its own land (Jung, 1970, para. 472). The Greek text Physiologus, associated with medieval theologist Epiphanius (310–403 CE) describes the resurrection of the phoenix. 'After it has lived for 500 years, it goes to the cedar forests of Lebanon and bathes in the fragrance from the trees, then signals the priest in the city of Heliopolis (the city of the sun), who prepares an altar. The phoenix flies to the city, alights on the altar, and ignites a fire that completely consumes it, leaving only ash. The next day the priest finds a worm in the ashes, on the second day a small bird, and on the third day the full-grown phoenix, completely renewed' (Plantin, 1588). The revival of the bird from a tiny worm (*vermes*), that Jung refers to in his writing of Epiphanius' Ancoratus, symbolizes transformation of inchoate matter into new life. The bird faces the sun as it ignites itself, signifying a death and resurrection process. The reference to flames and cinders alludes to a searing of flesh, a shrinking of bone and marrow and a reduction to ashes. Then a minuscule worm births from the ashes. The myth symbolizes journeys that are annihilating, where an individual may be destroyed after encountering a spate of fateful events. But for Phoolan, a young girl from a remote village of northern India, the ride was more than fateful.

This narrative describes actual events that took place in the decade of the eighties in an Indian village, polarized by caste, class and gender. Phoolan's story, drawn from a series of interviews by Marie-Therese

DOI: 10.4324/9780429423727-3

Cuny and Paul Rambali, is a recapitulation of her life, and also a commentary about a social world that had sunk into dark depths of anarchy. Several conflicting versions of Phoolan's life emerged following her imprisonment. I have followed Cuny and Rambali's account, based on oral interviews of Phoolan, which were transcribed and published with her approval (Devi, Cuny, and Rambali, 1997). It is the closest approximation of her life that we have today – a story of flesh, bones and ashes, new beginnings and then a reduction into ashes again.

Red Soil, a River, Neem Tree and Knife-Blade – The Flowering of Rage

Her name was Phoolan, and it meant flower. The village was near the ravines where, lower down in the plains, a perennial river flowed. Myth has it that the river, Yamuna, was the sister of Yama, the god of death. Phoolan's earliest memories were of the river. She remembered, because she played and swam in it, and crossed it to reach the land behind, where her parents tended a vegetable patch. But the path to the river was tricky, and the source of all her misery. The long way around the village was inconvenient, and the short way through her uncle's land, was forbidden. The old man chased children away, hurled abuses and thrashed Phoolan if she trespassed. It was the temptation of the pathway and her uncle's rage that set Phoolan thinking. Soon she found out that there was a conflict between her uncle and her father, Devdin. Bihari, her uncle, had seized her father's land, and the two were locked in a court battle. Devdin survived on odd jobs, and with a growing family and expenses at court, life was hard. The family lived in a tiny mud house at the far end of the village – the location was important, as it denoted their place in village hierarchy. They were Mallahs, a community of boatmen, who were the poorest and most exploited in that region.[1]

Devdin was a gentle and fearful man. He was frail, bent from long hours of work in the fields, and walks to the local courts. The dark-eyed Moola, Phoolan's mother, was quick-tempered, and cursed her fate endlessly for having four girls. Girls are considered a burden poor rural households, because their marriage claimed a bride-price (dowry), an arrangement that pushed men like Devdin into spiraling poverty. Though this practice has come under legislation in India since 1961 (Lodhia, 2022), the system of dowry continues to thrive in many parts of India. Girls are also sexually preyed upon, and Moola had to remind Phoolan often, to be careful of neighborhood men. But Phoolan was always in trouble. She trespassed through Bihari's property, plucked beans on neighboring farmlands, and missed her daily chores. There was never enough food in the house, she thought, and her father's tired, sad face worried her. Even a full day's work of collecting fodder, tending to crops and finishing chores did not bring in enough food to quell everyone's hunger.

Marriage was a way out, and plans were underway for the eldest girl Rukmini's wedding. Before Phoolan knew it, a match had been found for her too. She was only ten. An elderly widower had been chosen, in exchange of some money and cattle. But an incident before the wedding foreshadowed the ominous chain of events that were to follow. Bihari died suddenly, and his son Mayadin approached Devdin, for a truce. But when Devdin and Moola were away one night, Mayadin cut down an enormous, neem tree on their ancestral land. Phoolan rushed to the fields to see the tree fall, then charged fiercely at her cousin in protest. The tree had been Devdin's only hope – he had talked to Mayadin about using it for the girls' weddings. It made her hysterical. She tried to stop the men, clinging to the cart that was loading the wood, but her tiny body was no match for the group of men. The villagers watched in silence as the scene unfolded, and spoke later about the strange way Phoolan fought the men. Many years later, Phoolan re-membered the incident vividly. A powerful rage had erupted within her, which she had not known of before.

Her parents returned to discover Mayadin's betrayal, and while Moola cursed her fate, Devdin cowered in fear. It shocked Phoolan that they could do so little. On her wedding day, she was picked up from near the river, bathed and taken to the altar; when she looked at the man beside her, it was an old and ugly stranger named Putti Lal. Hungry, dazed, following little of what was happening around, she wished to go back to the riverbank. Devdin and Moolah objected to Putti Lal's demand of taking Phoolan away – she was a child, they said, and could be sent to him once she grew up. But like everything else that Devdin yielded to, his land, the neem tree, his brother's cruelty, he acceded to Putti Lal's demand. When Phoolan reached her hus-band's home, there was no family to greet her, and no women. When her father-in-law stepped outside one evening, her husband began assaulting her – he shoved and tossed her around, and finally took a knife-blade to cut her open. He said that it was a fun-game that married men indulged in. For days, she fought, hid herself, screamed for help and prayed that her parents would come to her rescue.

Terror Grounds

When her fevered and bruised body was discovered weeks later by her father, and brought back home, Moola's shock turned to fury. The fearful Devdin wept quietly, but would not confront Putti Lal. In the months following, Phoolan's fate was debated by village menfolk and the local council, in what was ostensibly a process of determining her future, since she had left her husband, they declared. Memories of Putti Lal haunted her, but the hours she spent near the river, and the warmth of her family restored her. She had become quiet and withdrawn, and would be angry whenever she went out with her father for daily work, and wages would be denied to them. Upper caste villagers exploited the poor by not paying them on time. Devdin worried about Phoolan's brashness, and her cousin Mayadin noted her growing aggression with displeasure.

Soon, she was being shunted back and forth between her husband and father, against Moolah's wishes. There were rumours in the village about her marriage, and attempts to get her remarried bore no results. Then one day, Moola was insulted by the village headman's daughter, and Phoolan retaliated. The conflict escalated and the headman felt antagonized. On a warm, sultry night when the family was resting, the headman's son, entered their house, and raped Phoolan at gunpoint. The terrified parents cried through her screams, fearing for their lives. The next day, broken and bruised, Phoolan began to plan revenge. A neighbouring village leader offered to help, and entered the headman's house to warn him. In retaliation, the headman, with the help of her cousin Mayadin, filed charges against Phoolan in the police station. She was hauled up in jail, where she was assaulted with boots, metal chairs, rods and bayonets and then raped. Devdin's painful sobs resounded from outside, but when Phoolan came out, she refused to speak. In the months that followed, she lived like a fugitive, hiding with distant relatives, trying to escape the headman's family and police. When she surfaced again, a rumor had spread that she had become a dacoit.

It was an eerie trail of events – of rage, revenge, vicious male strongholds and the dark entrails of poverty, caste oppression and lawlessness. Weeks later, a gang of upper caste men entered their house and raped her again. She was leered by neighbourhood women, and barred from drawing water from the community well. The men taunted Devidin, as his fifteen-year-old daughter became a nucleus of rapes, police brutality, caste wars and community proscription. Phoolan wished to die, but Moola would not let her. News about a feisty, headstrong low-caste girl named Phoolan, had spread. No one would give her work, and if Devdin found work, he would not be paid. Years later, she recalled that she had retreated into a shell, unable to talk, anxious, edgy, angry, sleepless and haunted. When villagers refused to pay her for work, she would charge violently. When a gang of dacoits abducted her shortly afterwards, she was surprised to see that they were not policemen or village overlords, but robbers and bandits from the valley. 'My hatred of men was so strong I desired only to be a man myself. I hated men, but all I wanted was to be like them, to have their power, and their freedom, to no longer be just flesh for them to toy with' (Devi, Cuny, and Rambali, 1997, p. 141). Taken into the ravines, she changed into men's attire, trekked large distances with the group, and learnt to shoot rifles. The changeover into a tough, gun-trotting outlaw, was aided by Vikram Mallah, the group's leader, whose lover and accomplice she became, eventually.

Through a slew of rapes, assaults, lootings and killings, Phoolan turned into the dreaded bandit she had been named as. In her account, she claimed that during her raids, she castrated rapists, robbed the rich and distributed money among the poor. When Vikram was killed in a gang-war, Phoolan was taken by rival gang-members, raped for days, paraded nude and left to die. After she recovered, she formed a new gang, then planned the massacre of seventeen upper caste Thakur men in Behmai, to avenge the assaults on her. The Behmai massacre put her on national radar, with a massive police hunt organized for her capture. Eventually, it led to her surrender and imprisonment. When everything of that violent and tumultuous life had been reduced to ashes, there crawled from within it a minuscule germ, from the remains of a broken and mutilated life. It was in the recollection of her life events, sharing of her innermost humiliations and wounds, that a link with the world was built again. In the ensuing years, Phoolan rebuilt herself, negotiated her release from prison, sought armed protection and accepted a political ticket to contest assembly elections. She rejected stories circulated about her, and narrated her own in specially commissioned interviews. A bridge was molded with the world through an outpouring of anguish, and through her recapitulations. She entered public life, and took up the cause of the oppressed. As a convicted criminal and dreaded killer, she was an unusual figure in Parliament. Not long after her political initiation and return to civilian life, Phoolan was gunned down by upper caste members of Behmai, in broad daylight in the capital city of Delhi. It was a sad end to a dark and tumultuous saga.

The Other – Social and Psychological Threads

Despite its horrific dimensions, Phoolan's case receded from public memory in a few decades. The rape and assault of twenty-two-year-old Jyoti Singh in New Delhi in December 2012, brought back a surge of protests against rapes. Jyoti Singh was raped in a moving bus, in the heart of India's metropolis, by a gang of five men, the youngest of whom was seventeen years old. She was hit and battered, her innards incised with metal rods, after which she was thrown off the bus on a highway, and left to die. Rapes are the most visible forms of violence that occur to women, globally. They are widespread and endemic, with global data showing their presence in all parts of the world, whatever the economic or geographical particulars.

In *On Violence and on Violence Against Women*, humanities scholar Jacqueline Rose writes about the violence that is invisible, that is the most insidious (Rose, 2021). Extreme hatred and desire to inflict pain is central to it, but its imperceptibleness is most significant, because the human capacity to harm is cloaked in self-blindness. The invisible nature of violence, Rose says, can be seen in silent legislations on abortion, in sexual abuse in power corridors, in thriving rape capitals of the world, where women are routinely burnt, disemboweled, hanged or shot. Rose links violence to colonial legacies, to racial and economic segregation, and notes how women take to violence, after violence has seared them. A 2003 American film *Monster* by Patty Jenkins dramatizes the life of serial killer Aileen Wuornos, a Florida street-prostitute, who murdered her male clients serially, claiming that they had tried to rape her (Jenkins, 2023). Wuornos was born to delinquent, teenage parents, who abandoned her after birth. She was sexually abused by her alcoholic grandfather, her caregiver, for years before she became a child-prostitute. Embroiled in self-harm and violence from early on, with no internalized attachment figures and no constituted self, Wuornos' fragile mental state produced a split-off, autonomous monster-like personality that led her to think that she was being raped by her male clients. The experience of abuse triggered violent defensive responses in her personality, inducing her acts of killing.

Phoolan, Jyoti Singh and Wuornos are not rare and isolated instances of female violence. The interiors of war-zones, international borders, disputed lands, execution camps, are places where rapes occur routinely, as also households, schools, farmlands, factories and care homes. A World Population review of 2022 shows countrywide rape statistics, and recounts the difficulties in statistical comparisons, with the parameters of rape being different across geographies. The report outlines various kinds of rapes and sexual violence. Even though most rapes go unreported, and the rise in numbers may indicate better reporting mechanisms and a broader definition of rape than actual increased incidences, the statistics is nonetheless intriguing. Australia, Sweden, Belgium, USA and UK are some of the developed nations in the world, with high reported incidences of rape, along with South Africa (World Population Review, 2022).

The Indian cases, both Phoolan and Jyoti's, raised an international outcry and were extensively broadcasted, documented and debated in the media. The film *Bandit Queen* was commissioned and funded by a British public television channel, as was the film on Jyoti Singh, titled *India's Daughter*. The serial rapes committed by Reynhard Sinaga in the United Kingdom, against heterosexual men, for which he was prosecuted in 2020, were no less macabre. Political science scholar Leela Fernandes notes that Phoolan's narrative(s), both oral and cinematic, depict Indian modernity as a failure, present Indian men and masculinity as destructive, and produce first-world representation of India as violent and disordered. Poverty and casteism reinforce the notion of the other, suggesting these nations to be inferior and corrupt, compared with so-called civilized, modern, democratized, advanced west (Fernandes, 1999). It is important to note the element of 'cultural othering' that Fernandes has identified, the splitting off of reprehensible parts on Asian and African nations. But given that rape and female sexual violence are global phenomena,

I wonder also if the massive interest generated in the Indian cases is because the issue impacts all. Phoolan's case showed police and local council's involvement in the assaults, and systemic violence on women.

I am bringing the social context in relation to the subject's internal world. Phoolan recalled her experiences of hunger, persecution and wounding, as well as the men who harmed her – her uncle Bihari, husband Putti Lal, the police, village headman, her cousin Mayadin, and the dacoits. She remembered her father's timidness, Vikram's affection and the feelings of hatred and affinity she felt for men. She remembered Moolah's anger, and the rapes after Vikram's death. The powerful, terrorizing quality of men, repelled and attracted her. She defended herself from the attacks but absorbed the same, dark, savage character herself. An alternate personality constellated, which none had seen before. The environment was crucial for this development, and caste dynamics was integral to it. Arundhati Roy's incisive account of how caste practices pervade Indian society is worth delving into. Roy unravels Gandhi's contentious stance about caste hegemony in India, and the constitutional expert B.R. Ambedkar's opposition to Gandhi, in a battle between two nationalist leaders, that reveal the underside of the Indian polity (Roy, 2014).

In *'The Rape that Woke up India: Hindu Imagination and the Rape of Jyoti Singh Pandey'* Mackenzie Brown and Nupur Agarwal trace the 2012 Delhi gang-rape of Jyoti Singh, and the pernicious face of rape in India (Brown and Agarwal, 2014). The authors do not claim rape to be a phenomenon exclusive to India, but trace the cultural, religious, social and institutional factors that contribute to gender violence in the subcontinent. They suggest that Vedic religious sagas portray women as abducted, abandoned or mutilated, and these shape the notion of feminine in culture. In surveys conducted by them to examine high incidences of sexual violence, factors of masculine aggression, women's growing independence, rape-tolerant attitudes, and inadequate police protection, were found to be key. Since Hindu myths also signify feminine potency and agency, mythic symbolization may not be actual incitements to rape, they concur. Nikki Bloch describes the images of rape in Ovid's *Metamorphosis*, the brutishness and misogyny of the gods, and the consequent suffering of women, narrated by the poet (Bloch, 2014). With cultural deterrents such as this, and effective vigilance mechanisms in western societies, gender violence has been pervasive. The authors refer to psychosocial aspects, fear and hatred of the feminine, endemic poverty and sexual repression, as contributing to a rape climate in India.

It is possible that psyche and social interact with each other to produce a cycle of violence, but that the instinctual psyche carries an insidious impulse to harm, as Jacqueline Rose suggests, is also important to consider. The founding theories of psyche were based on instincts and body (Kraft-Ebbing, Freud), but what is explored here, is an interpsychic realm, in which the self is constantly being shaped by acts that are directed against it. Jungian author Bradley T. Paske in *'Rape and Ritual: A Psychological Study'* describes rape and *death of the feminine* as correlated (Paske, 1982). Paske does not adopt a spiritualist notion of psyche in reaction to Freudian sexuality theories. Erotic desire is unrelated to the act of rape he says. We recall that Phoolan's rapists mentioned the word 'fun' in connection to the rapes, which alludes to an element of sadism. The interrelatedness of power, sex, pleasure and violence has been discussed in studies elsewhere (Gottschall, 2004; Winter, 2000; McPhail, 2016). McPhail argues that radical-liberal feminist perspectives of rape as an act of power and not sex do not fully explain the aetiology of rape. The perpetrator's background, such as childhood abuse, cognitive distortions, deviant sexual preferences, negative developmental experiences, lack of affection-based bonds with women, and feelings of inadequacy are key, in the role of sexuality in rape.

Michel Foucault's argument that rape needs to be desexualized in its criminalization, evoked strong reactions in feminist quarters in the seventies. Ann J. Cahill, phenomenological philosopher, has argued against Foucault's notion of the body as a functional entity that has no historical or cultural meaning. She states that the body is a social and cultural entity first, and desexualizing rape takes away the role that the body plays in feminine consciousness. There are many feminine bodies as there are experiences, and the embodied feminine is in a power discourse from the beginning, with feelings of fear, vulnerability and violability about her body in a male world. It is from the body that notions of resistance manifest, Cahill says (Cahill, 2000). In *'Psychoanalytic and Socio-Cultural Perspectives on Women in India'*, humanities scholar Supriya Chaudhuri writes about the global epidemic of violence and asks if the meaning of safety is an absence of harm or a suspension of threat (Chaudhuri, 2021). Citing instances of rape cases in India, Chaudhuri deliberates on the specific character of violence perpetrated against women. She notes its sociopathology in instances where 'incels' (involuntary celibates) routinely harbor violence against women and incite killings. Assault is experienced as pleasure, and pleasure is linked to the erotic and the feminine. Sexual violence, abduction and rape of women have been fundamental to how nations have formed world over, Chaudhuri writes – its range is spectral. In this sense, rape is experienced across a spectrum – in the body, in the notion of a violated self, in culture, and in its aftermath, where women's safety becomes a form of social tyranny, where the responsibility of safety is put on the victim, rather than the abuser.

Paske tells us that feminine promiscuity is discussed prominently in rape cases, and often the therapeutic attitude is that rape may have been provoked by the victim. While psycho-sexual factors would have been intrinsic to the rapes that Phoolan experienced, culture and environment played a crucial role. A powerful, male lobby was challenged when Phoolan rose against the village heads, police and other caste men. The assaults were part of caste, class and gender tensions. Paske says that the trauma of reliving the incident of rape, the victim's humiliation, anger, self-hatred and depression have a debilitating impact on the psyche. It can be imagined that Phoolan suffered all of it. A life-threatening experience could become a life-transforming one, if the emotional aftermath is addressed, Paske observes. Referring to Patricia Berry's archetypal take in 'The Demeter-Persephone Mythologem with Reference to Neurosis and Treatment' Paske describes how rape is an expression of the terrible dark mother Gaia, the chthonic feminine, who fulfills a particular telos in prompting her daughter's individuation through an encounter of the dark and archetypal other. He links this with Freud's view of the sexual realm and its instinctive depths, the unconscious *prima materia,* whose contents are never known. Loathing and dread of the feminine are part of it, as historically, women have been denoted as soulless, obscene, evil and mentally inferior, in many cultures.

In *Four Theories of Rape: A Macrosociological Analysis,* Larry Baron and Murray Straus look at rape from a sociological perspective and suggest that social disorganization is a key factor for increased female violence (Baron and Straus, 1987). Phoolan's rapes were committed within a highly hierarchized social world, with economic and political inequities. Jyoti Singh's rape involved migrant men living on the fringes of a thriving capital city, that has vast economic disparities between its residents. The authors write that a repressive gender climate, poverty and inequality, pornography and objectification of the female body, as well as remote rural locations promote incidences of rape. Feminist critics have linked explicit sexual visuals and pornography to a culture of gender inequality, while other studies have contested this and shown that pornography and gender equality have coexisted in some societies, and have not always produced high incidences of rape (Brod, 1988; Baron, 1990). Still, the complicity between the two seems disconcerting.

These sociological pointers, are important but provisional, since there are aspects about rape that are still unclear – for instance, the individual's capacity to commit violence. Hatred and abhorrence of the feminine that Paske outlines, and the impulse for violence in the human psyche, that Rose highlights, are important factors. The extreme violence that Phoolan encountered constellated a powerful personality in her – combative, dangerous and vengeful. Jung notes that contra-sexual entities are unconscious complexes, and the autonomous complex is of an unknown nature. A man is possessed by complexes, and a possessed man resembles the picture of a hysterical woman, the anima (Jung, 1966, para. 387). The men involved in the rapes were filled with unconscious hatred towards Phoolan, even before she became a frenzied, tyrannical figure herself. Jung's comment, that only women reflect a hysterical personality, is again, misplaced characterization of the feminine.

Dualities, Dissensions, Intersexuality and Feminine Otherness

Phoolan's dissent was an aberration in her milieu – women were not known to protest in their subordinate positions in that collective. The power and powerlessness of men that she experienced around her, evoked in her conflicting feelings about them. Her abduction severed the last links that she had with her family. An alternate personality emerged in her then - the outer separation induced an inner dissociation, and the emergence of a new personality. Life in bandit-land, away from her village, shaped the inner other, whose rudimentary expression was savage and demonic. It was distinct from the young and innocent girl who loved the riverside, went to work and tended to household chores. Jung said that when the complex is split off, and reaches an organic structure, the dissociation leads to a psychosis or a schizophrenic condition, where the split-off complex has a life of its own, with nothing to tie it to the rest of the personality (Jung, 1955, para. 382). Phoolan's massacre of villagers at Behmai was an expression of a dark dissociative complex that had constellated in her, from the trauma of multiple rapes.

Yet, away from her family, in the harsh and grueling ravines, memories of her parents and siblings surfaced often, and reminded her of a time back home. When she could no more take the fear of being apprehended by the police or killed by rival gangs, Phoolan decided to surrender. On being asked, as to how she developed the ingenious capacity to comb the ravines and survive as an outlaw, she remarked that it was the goddess who imbued her with a mysterious power. The psychological complex has a demonic force, and functions autonomously when it is split from the ego. The transitional states that Phoolan experienced, from a frail, oppressed village girl to a dreaded dacoit, and then an articulate public figure, reflected a long journey, inner and outer. She remarked that she had surrendered, but not to the police, since the police had raped her, and she would not bow before them. Her return to civilian life was a self-restorative act. Although she was murdered subsequently, it was not before she had exposed the dark underside of her social world. Hers was the first public account in India of the close nexus between rape, gender, caste oppression and poverty – an exposé that broke the silence around rapes and the insidious face of patriarchy.

This narrative is not only an instance of how the feminine is othered in culture, but also a vivid account of Phoolan's transformation from a marginalized feminine to an empowered public persona. A daemonic Phoenix-like force constellated in her, and helped her rise each time she was crushed. The fierceness of her instincts matched the aggressive forces that she fought.

It took her several years in prison, to disengage from its malignant energy, and retrieve her sense of Self. The first sign of her nascent agency was her angry protest when she saw the ancestral tree being felled. Its ferocity surprised her. She remarked later that she was born with her mother's anger. The tree was a symbol of her family, the integrity of the parental unit, and also her yet undeveloped Self. In the years following, Phoolan experienced pain and rage over and over again. It was evoked, whenever she narrated her story to her interviewers. The long recapitulation had a confessional quality; it clarified her mind, allowing her to recall the darkest phases of her childhood. Her journey revealed a recurrent pattern – hostile encounters with men. From Bihari's outbursts, Putti Lal's knifing, Mayadin's treachery, the rapist police and village heads, Phoolan was embroiled with the dark and destructive masculine from childhood. Her maturation involved a reorienting of her feelings about power, from a mimetic enactment of violence to careful deliberation. It is inconceivable how any kind of psychological healing was possible for Phoolan, given the scale of violence she faced. But she turned her experience into a social and political cause, showing astonishing boldness and astuteness in entering public life. Her recovery and restitution were the most moving elements of her story.

In a workshop on body and the unconscious that I conducted many years back, a colleague shared a dream that she had the night before. In the dream, she had seen herself fully clothed getting ready for work, when all of a sudden, her dress flared up, exposing her lower body. To her embarrassment and amusement, she saw that the exposed part of her body had an erect phallus. The description of the dream led me to research it, and to my surprise, I found an exact representation of the image in an ancient Greek sculpture of Aphroditus, a masculine rendition of Aphrodite (Figure 3.1).

In *Gender, Identity and Body*, Rosemary Barrow writes that the indefiniteness of gender identities was expressed in Hellenistic representations of the body (Barrow, 2018). The female body underwent many revisions, from soft curves to fleshy and muscular contours, with gods like Dionysius and Apollo portrayed as beardless, long-haired and full-cheeked. Hermaphroditic representations in ancient Greek sculptures show the disruption and blurring of gender binaries, and the presence of a visible intersex body. Hermaphroditus, the child of Hermes and Aphrodite, was a central figure in this tradition, actively worshipped as a fertility symbol. The worship of *anasyromenos* statues, the image of a phallic feminine or female body with a phallus, was a cult practice in ancient Greece. Barrow writes, 'Taking their name from the verb *anasuresthai* ("to pull up one's clothing"), these statuettes depict draped feminized figures with breasts. Dressed in a high-belted chiton, they pull up their drapery to the hip to reveal a penis beneath that is often erect. The gesture sets the viewer up for a shock, when (like the god Pan on the Pompeian wall painting) we see a male organ, not the female organ we were expecting'

FIGURE 3.1 Aphroditus.

Source: Carole Raddato, CC BY-SA 2.0, via Wikimedia Commons, https://commons.wikimedia.org/wiki/File:National_Archaeological_Museum_of_Spain,_Madrid_(15456930062).jpg

(Barrow, 2018, p. 80). The god Pan was aghast to discover that the nymph he was pursuing was a hermaphrodite. This bewilderment is something similar to what the dreamer felt when she saw herself in the dream with an exposed phallus, or the feelings of bemusement in the collective, when Phoolan first emerged in public eye. She had lifted a veil, and revealed a powerful masculine body beneath her frail frame, that had survived a sea of assaults. It was the image of a non-conforming feminine.

The *anasyromenos* statue evokes early notions of transgenderism, but psychologically, it suggests the ambivalence and polarities contained in contrasexuality. These mythic abstractions convey the reluctance to portray the feminine as fixed and singular, and the multiple selves that the feminine inheres in its otherness. In *Celebrating the Phallus* Warren Colman notes the extreme positions of biological determinism and cultural relativism in current debates on gender, sexuality and psyche (Colman, 2001). Undermining sexual differences, that in turn produce different psychological experiences for men and women, points to mind-body split, he says. I would add that women experience their bodies not in terms of sexual drives alone, but also in their reproductive powers, in their hard labor and extreme vulnerability. In rural India, women struggle with impoverishment and burdened life conditions. In the western Indian state of Rajasthan for instance, rural women trek for hours across deserts to fetch water from far-off wells, exposing themselves to harsh weather and threat of rapes. While they combine household work with daily wage labor, they enjoy almost no economic and political power. The lived experience of the feminine in these settings is in hunger, violence, toil, lack of reproductive choices and access to resources – universal in many parts of the developing world. The archetypal male is despised, dreaded, desired, envied, in shifting emotions of hatred and longing, in complex socio-cultural dynamics of gender, poverty and oppression.

Colman points out the creative and destructive aspects of the symbolic phallus, its monstrosity and its mystical, and generative aspects. The role of sexual fantasies in the formation of masculine identity is important he says, with differentiation from the mother as primary in it. The differentiation from the mother implies also a mature affinity with the feminine, not a dissociation and severance. The latter induces a climate of hatred and violence towards the feminine other, which Phoolan experienced in her environment.

The dream of an *anasyromenos* figure points to phallic feminine, or feminine subjectivity that transcends binaries of gender. The body was at the center of Phoolan's many-faceted personality. The body that tended to housework and daily labor in the village, and the body that scaled the ravines and fielded guns. Phoolan's dissentious spirit, her refusal to be intimidated by Bihari and Mayadin, choosing to be with Vickram Mallah and her act of revenge in the Behmai massacre, had risen from the same body – multiple in its subjectivity. Dissent and aggression are not essentially masculine, but in the collective she grew up, feminine and masculine perceptions were fixed, and Phoolan's courage and will were singular.

There are many ways in which the other reveals itself. American poet, essayist Adrienne Rich (1929–2012) found that experience of marriage and motherhood in a regressive heterosexual world, radicalized her sexual and political identity as a lesbian. Rich did not face economic and caste oppression, nor did she encounter male violence in the eclectic intellectual world she inhabited, but she witnessed silent oppression in her mother's life, and felt it in her own marriage, in her tedious, domestic womanly existence. It led her to examine her location and relationship with the world, and an awakening into otherness, that first manifested in her body in physical ailments in early childhood (Doherty, 2020).

Rich's conflictual relation with the feminine world and alienation from it fuelled her struggle with her own identity. It led her to discover an alternate being within her, that she believed would never be fully knowable. Living in a patriarchal, heterosexual world, Rich engaged with her otherness, her multiple selves and unfolding identity, using her incisive writing to protest against the system (Slowick, 1984). The inner other was in tension with the outer environment where heterosexuality, war and racism, were predominant. Rich's ideological differences with the world served as a ground for the emergence of a new self, and offered a contra-sexual apparatus in her individuation. Exploring intimate relations within same gender, using creative techniques, venturing into activism, Rich experienced her feminine otherness in relation to the world, remaining in conflict and dialogue with it. Much of it, like Phoolan, was experienced in the body, as it was in the mind. The extraordinarily different pathways that individuals follow reaffirm not just the fluidity of the feminine, but the peculiarity and uniqueness of each individuating journey. Both Phoolan and Rich's narratives are marked by feminine emergence, in distinct experiences of contra-sexuality. It is not the psyche alone that determines this, but the psyche in relation to culture. When looked at from a psychological standpoint, the subject's non-conformist behaviour seems problematic. When seen in relation to history, and the individual's location in a social world, a dialectical tension is noted, where women are seen encountering conflicts within the collective. The archetype is indistinctly grasped without this relational outer realm, since it is the environment where notions of masculine and feminine are shaped, and where gender forces are encountered.

In a discussion about the idea of India, historian Romila Thapar and feminist literary scholar Gayatri Chakravorty Spivak dwell on the fixity and stasis of ideas, or how fixed ideas prevent multiplicities of meaning to emerge. The concept of India, they say, is not a fixed idea but rather multiple images of India in its Hindu and Islamic history, ancient and colonial pasts, Marxist and socialist politics, subaltern consciousness, freedom struggle, its languages and subcultures within an overarching nationhood, all of which makes it impossible to have a uniform and fixed idea of India (History for Peace, 2017). There is also an India with caste and religious conflicts. I would think the idea of feminine contra-sexuality is similarly oriented – plural, ambivalent and multiple. Although Jung advocated multiplicity of meaning in archetypal images, his notions of contra-sexual animus and the feminine did not reveal the diversity of the archetype.

Note

1 Caste – A system of social hierarchy in India that segregates individuals based on family of birth, and occupation. The highest is the priestly caste, followed by castes of warriors and then traders. There are many subcastes under the four main castes. The lowest caste is formed of servicemen. Caste system follows practices of purity/impurity and endogamy, and is active in many parts of India. There are in-depth sociological studies in India on caste and its prevalence. The constitution of India guarantees support of weaker sections of society and protection of economically and socially disadvantaged people, and prohibits discrimination against any citizen on the basis of caste, religion, sex or gender. But the caste system continues to subsist in insidious ways in India. The Indian Constitution committee was headed by Dr. B.R. Ambedkar, himself a member of the Dalit caste.

References

Baron, L. (1990) 'Pornography and Gender Equality: An Empirical Analysis', *The Journal of Sex Research*, 27(3), pp. 363–380.

Baron, L. and Straus, M. (1987) 'Four Theories of Rape: A Macrosociological Analysis', *Social Problems*, 34(5), pp. 467–448.

Barrow, R. (2018) 'The Indefinite Body: Sleeping Hermaphrodite', Chapter 5 in *Gender, Identity and the Body in Greek and Roman Sculpture*. Cambridge: Cambridge University Press, pp. 76–88.

Bloch, N. (2014) *Patterns of Rape in Ovid's Metamorphosis*. Undergraduate Honors thesis, Department of Classics, University of Colorado, Boulder.

Brod, H. (1988) 'Pornography and the Alienation of Male Sexuality', *Social Theory and Practice*, 14(3), Special Issue: Marxism Feminism: Powers of Theory/Theories of Power, pp. 265–284.

Brown, M. C. and Agarwal, D. N. (2014) 'The Rape that Woke Up India', *Trinity University Source: Journal of Religion and Violence*, 2(2), pp. 234–280.

Cahill, A. J. (2000) 'Foucault, Rape, and the Construction of the Feminine Body', *Hypatia*, 15(1), pp. 43–63.

Chaudhuri, S. (2021) '"Marked Unsafe": Women, Violence, and the State of Risk', in Ellman, P. L., Basak, J., and Schlessinger-Kipp, G. (eds.), *Psychoanalytic and Socio-Cultural Perspectives on Women in India: Violence, Safety and Survival*. London: Routledge, pp. 20–32.

Colman, W. (2001) 'Celebrating the Phallus' in Harding, C. (ed.), *Sexuality. Psychoanalytic Perspectives*. Hove & Philadelphia: Bruner-Routledge, pp. 121–136.

Devi, P., Cuny, M., and Rambali, P. (1997) *I, Phoolan Devi: The Autobiography of India's Bandit Queen*, 2nd ed. London: Sphere.

Doherty, M. (2020) 'The Long Awakening of Adrienne Rich', *The New Yorker*, November 30, p. 2020.

Fernandes, L. (1999) 'Reading "India's Bandit Queen": A Trans/national Feminist Perspective on the Discrepancies of Representation', *Signs*, 25(1), pp. 123–152.

Gottschall, J. (2004) 'Explaining Wartime Rape', *The Journal of Sex Research*, 41(2), pp. 129–136.

History for Peace. (2017) 'The Idea of India: Romila Thapar and Gayatri Chakravorty Spivak in Conversation'. 3rd Annual History for Peace Conference, ICCR, August 14. https://www.historyforpeace.pw/post/the-idea-of-india-romila-thapar-and-gayatri-chakravorty-spivak-in-conversation.

Jenkins, J. P. "Aileen Wuornos." *Encyclopedia Britannica*, April 26, 2023. https://www.britannica.com/biography/Aileen-Wuornos

Jung, C. G. (1955) *The Symbolic Life: Miscellaneous Writings,* Vol. 18, The Collected Works of C. G. Jung. Princeton, NJ: Princeton University Press.

Jung, C. G. (1970) *Mysterium Coniunctionis,* Vol. 14, The Collected Works of C. G. Jung. Princeton, NJ: Princeton University Press.

Jung, C. G. (1966) *Two Essays in Analytical Psychology*, Vol. 7, The Collected Works of C. G. Jung. Princeton, NJ: Princeton University Press.

Lodhia, S. (2022) 'Dowry Prohibition Act', *Encyclopedia Britannica*, October 7.

McPhail, A. B. (2016) 'Feminist Framework Plus: Knitting Feminist Theories of Rape Etiology into a Comprehensive Model', *Trauma, Violence & Abuse*, 17(3), pp. 314–329.

Paske, B. (1982) *Rape and Ritual: A Psychological Study*. Ontario: Inner City Books.

Plantin, C. (1588) *Sancti Epiphanii ad Physiologum*. Available at Special Collections, McPherson Library, University of Victoria, https://spcoll.library.uvic.ca/Digit/physiologum/index.html.

Rose, J. (2021) *On Violence and on Violence against Women*. New York: Farrar, Straus and Giroux.

Roy, A. (2014) *The Doctor and the Saint: The Ambedkar-Gandhi Debate – Caste, Race and Annihilation of Caste*. India, Penguin/Random House.

Slowick, M. (1984) 'The Friction of the Mind: The Early Poetry of Adrienne Rich', *The Massachusetts Review*, 25(1), pp. 142–160.

Winter, D. (2000). 'Power, Sex, and Violence: A Psychological Reconstruction of the 20th Century and an Intellectual Agenda for Political Psychology', *Political Psychology*, 21(2), pp. 383–404.

World Population Review (2022) '2022 World Population by Country', https://worldpopulationreview.com

4

THE CLAY GODDESS

Cultural Tensions in Postcolonial Thought

In his thirty-odd years of engagement with India between 1930 and 1961, Jung affirmed a Tagorean premise that transcultural experiences elicit more difference and divergence, than uniformity and unity. 'Uniformity is not unity ... Those who destroy the independence of other races, destroy the unity of all races of humanity' (Tagore, 1921, p. 540). Knowledge as a heterodoxic pursuit that is involved with other enterprises of knowledge and other cultures, has been known in India since long.[1] Citing how its reverse was advocated by philosophers like James Mill (1773–1836), noted economist and philosopher, Amartya Sen says that Mill's views of India revealed as much about British imperialist attitudes, as it did about Indian history (Sen, 2001).

Sen notes that in *The History of British India* (1818), Mill summarily rejected all claims about Indian epistemology, and reproached British orientalists like William Jones for advocating the sophistry of ancient Indian texts. 'Mill was particularly dismissive of the alleged scientific and mathematical works in India. He denied the generally accepted belief that the decimal system (with place values and the placed use of zero) had emerged in India, and refused to accept that Aryabhata and followers could have had anything interesting to say on the diurnal motion of the earth and the principles of gravitation' (Sen, 2001, p. 11). Mill's rather dim evaluation of the east (in which he clubbed Chinese, Persian, Japanese, Burmese, Tibetans cultures) was in direct contrast to Iranian scholar Al-Biruni's *Tārīkh al-Hind* (1017 CE), a history of India in Arabic that describes mathematical and astronomical theories formulated in ancient India. Unlike Mill, Al-Biruni learnt Sanskrit, and studied Indian science, during his Indian sojourn (Khan, 1976; Mishra, 1979).

DOI: 10.4324/9780429423727-4

In '*India: What Can it Teach Us?*', Max Mueller writes that he had to discourage British students (routinely examined on Mill's *The History of British India* before they took up administrative tenure in India) from reading Mills' volume, due to its inaccurate and incomplete descriptions about India (Mueller, 1882, 2007).

Jung's engagement with India happened at a time when cultural and historical worlds were vastly contrasted. The east had evolved a variety of religious traditions, while the west had experienced Enlightenment, and witnessed the growth of scientific reason. When parts of east were still under colonial dominance, western nations had undergone two major wars and witnessed the birth of scientific psychology. The birth of empirical psychology has distinct links with the cultural and political history of west. Jung ventured beyond conventional boundaries of psychoanalytic knowledge in pursuing his interests in eastern philosophy and religion. Though not the only one, his is the only known history of a psychoanalyst's sustained engagement with Indian thought. This was not merely because transcultural symbols and the collective unconscious were objects of his inquiry, but also because the east had developed perspectives about consciousness that aroused Jung's interest. What Sen and Tagore both underscore about knowledge is heterogeneity, rather than uniformity and dominance of single worldviews.

In *Moses and Monotheism* (1939), Freud differentiated polytheistic faiths from Jewish religion, by characterizing the former as primitive and inferior, in their adherence to God images, sun worship, concept of afterlife, magic and sorcery. The abstraction of one God, whose image should not be made, nor his name breathed, was considered supreme (Freud, 1939, p. 33). Earlier, in *Totem and Taboo*, Freud said that religious phenomenon had to be understood from the point of human neurosis, since memories of obscure, 'golden' past evoke spells of magical childhood, and helps displace present discontent to a grandiose past. (Freud, 1913). Myths reveal more about the genesis of human neurosis and psychopathology, than about a real heroic age, he said. These are important observations, and while idealization is not uncommon in evocations of the past, is the archaic made up entirely of idealized wholes? Conflict and dissension were conspicuous among ancients, actively encouraged even, particularly in the philosophical schools of India, and heroic sagas more often than not revealed murkiness of human world than perfected and accomplished lives.

Jung's take on antiquity was different. He told Joseph Henderson on his return from India in 1938, that he saw the religions of the East as a great challenge to western psychotherapy (Coward, 1985, p. xii). Aside from transcultural symbols which gave him indications about the collective unconscious, the east gave Jung an Archimedean standpoint about his own work (Sengupta, 2022, p. 117). In '*What India Can Teach Us*', Jung remarked that encountering a culture where thought and instinct are not separate, and where evil could be found symbolized in sacred temple sites, were edifying experiences, especially for an outsider cloaked in notions of moral superiority (Jung, 1970).

The Archaic

In these mixed appraisals of India, the notion of archaic has remained a contested one. Cultural psychologist Ashis Nandy says that colonization of knowledge and the impulse towards universalism have minimized possibilities of integrating traditional knowledge with mainstream thought. It is not just classics that remain outside mainstream discourse, but indigenous narratives that face the prospect of being taken out of their unique lived contexts, in order to be theorized (Nandy and Darby, 2018). A Hegelian approach of 'the rational alone is real', and primacy of written texts, encourage rejection of indigenous knowledge systems, symbolic material and oral traditions. Parallelly, phrases like 'half savage, half child' perpetrate racist and colonialist attitudes in transcultural discourse. Nandy contends that hegemonic structures and colonialist perspectives internalized by subordinated minds are more dangerous than domination itself. For Jungian analyst Wolfgang Giegerich, the logical interiorization of the soul in a disenchanted modernity, or the psyche as separate from natural sciences, metaphysics and theology, devoid of archaic remnants, is the only viable psychological truth we can claim for ourselves today (Giegerich, 2012). This last, pushes culture, especially indigenous cultures and mnemonic traditions outside the realm of psychological discourse.

Classical scholar Paul Bishop writes that the archaic is not just a chronological category or a primordial entity, but a quality of thought that is prelogical (Bishop, 2012, pp. 226–232). Bishop clarifies that Jung's idea of archaic does not imply a mystical realm, but a psychic function that is devoid of a subject-object divide. The prelogical aspect of the archaic is its conception of inner and outer as unbroken. Archaic and modern are therefore two kinds of thinking, the subject-object difference characterizing modern attitude, and unity with natural world characterizing archaic thought. Interrogating the notion of archaic is critical. The perceived unity of inner and outer in the archaic, does not imply an erasure of differences. The two Indian epics show very divergent views about the human world. In one, the non-human world is the locus of evil, while in the other, evil is personified among members of a royal clan, and in fraternal rivalry. In one epic, victory over evil marks the beginning of a new era of kingship, while in the other, the war brings an apocalyptic end to the human world. In classical Indian philosophy, notions of God, death and afterlife, human suffering and action, have been argued from reverse ontologies in Carvaka and Samkhya traditions. The archaic is a repository of many worldviews, that are conflicting rather than homogenous. Rejecting our links with the past, claiming that the psyche is located only in the present, in a logical, ahistorical, acultural realm of interiority, in secluded western enclaves, is problematic.

Religious Studies and myth scholar Robert Segal says that theories about myths (he argues that myths have no theory of their own) revolve around questions of origin, function and content. Segal defines myths as stories about gods, humans and animals, and their existential forebodings and anxieties. Levi-Strauss's theory of myths, as stories of opposition and their resolution, is one approach. Freud's concept of the Oedipus complex as repressed parental desires or unconscious castration anxieties is another (Segal, 2004). Jung's use of myths, in comparison, involves not one dominant myth or psychological precept, but the notion of archetypes. While Freud emphasized universal application of the Oedipus myth, Jung's archetypes, though deemed universal, are many-sided, and suggest not just repressed sexual contents, but psychic oppositions and dualities. The complex dynamics of the unconscious psyche is best expressed through mythic motifs, Jung felt. Myths in Jungian theory, necessitate an understanding of archetypes. What follows here, from archetypes, are not myths of Vedic theogony per se, but mythic evocations of the feminine in lived experiences of culture.

Cultural Particulars

In discussing the notion of feminine with Freudian scholar Livio Boni, cultural psychologist Ashis Nandy distances himself from Jungian archetypes, and from what is purportedly Jung's notion of an essential, universal feminine (Nandy, 2021). Nandy refers to radical feminine metaphors instead, and thinks that Jung's allusion to primaeval symbols and the feminine imbued with creative and destructive powers are more useful to consider. Disengaging from Jung's notion of archetypes because of its universal connotations, is fairly routine in psychoanalytic discourse. In the *Routledge Handbook of Psychoanalysis,* psychoanalytic philosopher Adrian Johnston refers to Freud and Lacan's repudiation of Jung's ideas, for his '(spiritualistic metaphysical realism of the transhistorical archetypes)', saying that 'Freudian-Lacanian analysis does not subscribe to classical metaphysical realism (with its universal and immaterial forms)'. (Elliott and Prager, 2016, p 290) Johnston thinks that the opposition between metaphysical realism and nominalism, is as longstanding as the schism between an enchanted, religious world and an irreligious, scientific and materialist one. In the same volume, psychoanalytic psychologist Janet Sayers discusses feminist history of psychoanalysis, and refers to Freud's rejection of Jung's notion of preconceived symbols, and interpretation of dreams based on symbolic meaning (Elliott and Prager, 2016, p. 421). She says that while feminists have been disenchanted with psychoanalysis for theorizing women's psychology without consideration of differences in history, ethnicity, social class, disability, sexual orientation, etc., symbolism is not a recourse. Feminists find difference and de-universalism in the work of Jacques Derrida and Michel Foucault, more significant instead (Elliott and Prager, 2016, p. 417).

In *Freud and Culture*, Eric Smadja discards Jung's notion of archetypes and collective unconscious, while acceding Freud's ideas of *Kulturarbeit,* or the impact of social phenomenon on the construction of human psyche (Smadja, 2015). Culture as humanization of the individual, through repression of instincts and transformation of narcissistic impulses, are ideas that Smadja links to Freud's influences from his Viennese Jewish upbringing. He omits myths and religious metaphors, thereby excluding vast resources of knowledge in traditional cultures where myths and symbols are primary modes of ex-pression for inner subjective contents. The unconscious, made up of repressed instinctual contents is separated from the psyche that has archaic symbols and religious signifiers that are used to express the subject's inner, subjective world. Consequently, archetypes, polytheistic symbols and archaic constituents are rejected in favor of rational, concretist material. This reinforces (like Mill's history of India) hegemonic views about cultures, where the other may be psychologized upon, but not engaged with, in its complexity, contrast and difference. As the Indian myth of the clay goddess reveals, not only is the notion of contra-sexuality contained in archaic thought, but instances of how contra-sexual dualities play out in culture are also evident in con-temporary narratives. Rather than universalist and essentialist meaning of archetypes, the myths reveal multiplicity of meaning.

The concept of psychological unconscious that evolved from post-Enlightenment thought, is unique to the intellectual history of west (Ellenberger, 1981; Shamdasani, 2003). While Jung's intellectual interests were fostered in this tradition, his disenchantment with Christian dogmas led him to explore alternate cultural traditions. This took him outside western materialist science. With respect to the unconscious, Jung's concern was the soul, and the psyche that was alienated from the soul (Jung, 2018). He contended that the unconscious was not just made of repressed personal instincts, but had ancestral vestiges, psychic substrate of a suprapersonal nature that were beyond feeling-toned complexes. Recurrent mythic motifs in his patients' dreams, indicated the presence of archaic vestiges in the unconscious. These were not of personalistic nature, he said, but had collective implications (Jung, 1969).

Jung proposed a few pointers about archetypes. Archetypal imagery had to be approached not causally, but through pre-causal and imagistic modes of thought. When constellated, archetypal contents induce affective mental states, and feelings of *mysterium fascinosum.* Being autonomous and imbued with affective energy, archetypes need to be brought into consciousness, and not identified with, as the latter could lead to possession.

The primary thrust of Jung's theory of archetype is its autonomous and affective character. Recent studies have affirmed that archetypes constellate in the individual psyche through interactions within brain, instinct, environment, teleology and personal history. For instance, symbols of mother, father, child, etc., have shared significance across cultures, but their constellation in the individual psyche renders the archetype with personal significance. Archetypes have dual, paradoxical, compensatory and unifying drives. While they may emerge in personal unconscious, environment and cultural particulars are critical for assimilating their meaning. The myths narrated in this volume do not evoke an archaic that has receded from imagination, but myths as performative traditions that are extant in culture.

Durga, Dopdi and Fierce Narratives of the Feminine

It is that time of the year when tracts of willowy *kash* (*Saccharum spontaneum*) can be seen near riversides, and sounds of drumbeats are heard from afar. The month of *Ashvin* is auspicious in Vedic calendar.[2] The air is soaked with the fragrance of jasmines, altars are strewn with flowers and assorted objects, and the floors are adorned with mystical drawings. The goddess is embodied in myths and folklores of the land, in food and hearth and in numerous rituals of worship performed within homes. But her real traces are in the women who tend to these homes, their cheerful and sad faces veiling countless stories of rising and falling. Women who toil in distant towns and cities, their bodies worn out from labor, but spirits still unbroken.

The myth of the goddess spans a transcendent whole. The female body has many potencies, from desire, dissent, capacity to labor and care. It is the body which is imagined when memories of the goddess surface – richly draped, mounted on a lion, arms spearing a demon. Scores of male potters in an old city quarter named *Kumartoli* in Kolkata, sculpt her form from riverside clay, paint her in luminous hues and embellish her with jewels. Thousands gather yearly to celebrate a myth, centuries old. In those hours and days, the goddess seems incarnated in every being, radiating in all who have gathered around her. It is not the veracity of the myths that concerns anyone, but the emotions they are evoked in the collective as the festivities unfurl.

Myth has it that a cruel, power-crazy demon performed many sacrifices to ask Brahma for a boon of immortality (Bhattacharji, 1995). When that was not granted, he asked that he be killed only by a woman. Believing this to be impossible, the demon began tormenting everyone and seized dominion of all three worlds. The gods were forced to confer and find a way out of this predicament, and it was then that Durga was conceived. The benign and beautiful Parvati, Shiva's consort, was imbued with battle prowess and transformed into a fearless, potent figure named Durga. It is a mythical trope that suggests the liminality of the archetype, and its fluid and shifting nature.

The transmuted goddess radiates fury and grace, a numinous vision that draws thousands of people to festival grounds during the autumnal season. On an illumined podium, is a surreal tableau of clay sculptures – embellished, exaggerated and primeval. An assortment of arms and crests adorns the goddess. Amongst these, a trident from Shiva that can impale flesh and impart consciousness, a conch shell that signifies victory, a lethal battle disc gifted by Vishnu, the ubiquitous lotus, symbol of wisdom, sword, bow and arrow, mace and axe, a thunderbolt from Indra and finally, a snake that marks her consort's muted presence. Celebrated annually, the event is inscribed in UNESCO's Representative List as an 'intangible cultural heritage of humanity'.[3]

The numinosity of the image stems from its play of opposites. The luxuriously draped goddess is crafted by male artisans and mounted on a maned beast, and the gory battle scene is tempered by the presence of her family. Crests of creation are juxtaposed with weapons, and sombre rites of worship are accompanied by bonhomie and celebration – an elaborate trope, built around opposites. Although the goddess radiates a fierce expression as she spears the demon, the battle scene is softened by the presence her young children. The recurrent choral incantations of 'mother' during the worship suggest a maternal enthrallment in the collective (Kakar, 2003), evident also in the four neo-adult children, who appear spellbound by her. Their presence seems intended to orient them to age-old conflicts of good and evil. Parental idealizations are as old as millennial myths. Durga's warlike attitude is offset by her exquisite grace, and although she is a creation of the male gods, she appears independent, imbued with unknown, autonomous powers. Finally, it is not what she is, but what her image evokes in the collective, and the enormous hold mythic enactments have on collective consciousness. The festival has both secular and religious undertones, and it is this duality between sacred and commonplace, faith and fantasy, that renders it timeless.

In *The Hour of the Goddess*, writer and translator Chitrita Banerji describes how food, worship, music, art and ecology come together to produce a feminine metaphor in Bengal that is composite in its wholeness. (Banerji, 2006) The goddess is evoked in crop cycles and seasons, in flora and fauna, in music and poetry and in arcadian traditions of the land. She is linked to the non-human world, symbolized in conjugal love and maternal care, portrayed in images of combat and peace, and in all kinds of harmonizing opposites. Ancient rites are evoked in her worship; the element of participation mystique is dominant. A sacred hour in autumn announces the beginning of the festival, and a carnivalesque rite enacted on the tenth day of the calendar, marks a closure. Married women smear vermillion on each other on the concluding day, break into ululations, following which the clay figures are ceremoniously immersed in river. They are molded the following autumn, from the same loamy riverbed soil. Dissolving and emerging from the earth, the goddess lingers on in collective imagination, and comes alive in stories of the land, stories of chaos and rising.

It is imaginable that such a cultural kaleidoscope impacts the subjective world of the individual in subliminal ways, in aversion to religious rituals, indifference or adherence to the sacred. The image of a female terracotta figurine from ancient Mohenjo-Daro civilization, shows the animism, chthonic potency and gravitas of the clay goddess (Figure 4.1). Her cyclical emergence and disintegration suggests transience of the human world, as also its fluidity. The radiant Durga is a contrast to the dark goddess Kali, who wreaks havoc when provoked. They belong to a group of mother goddesses, that embody creative and destructive aspects of the feminine. Kali is a symbol of an irate and agitated feminine, who is harassed by demons. She regains her composure when Shiva obstructs her path by lying before her, a contact that helps her retrieve her conscious attitude. Durga too is supported by her consort, but unlike Kali, she is composed in battle.

In *Critical Humanities from India,* cultural and literary scholar D. Venkat Rao writes about mnemonic impulses and biocultural formations that keep indigenous inheritances alive, through performative rituals, sonic-melodic forms and visual imageries (Rao, 2018). The acoustic and graphic traditions cannot be textualized, he says, embodied as they are in archaic forms. Mnemonic inheritances like myths, rituals and performative acts, reveal cultural formations that are more than a millennium old. Rao says that these unstructured memories, supplement written texts and constitute large mnemonic knowledgebases in ancient cultures. He assigns key attributes to mnemonic accents – allusion, citation, numeration, melopoeia and reasoning imagination (Rao, 2018, pp. 208–220). It is what classicist Paul Bishop would describe as prelogical thought, or what Jung would term, imagistic and pre-causal. Figural thinking, melodic enactments, allusion, the notion of the other, ritual enactments are central in these reconstituted memories. Venkat (like Nandy) remains concerned about locating these cultural formations outside colonialist, hegemonic paradigms and legacies of universalism. Jungian scholar Susan Rowland articulates something similar, in Jung's religious and cultural impulses outside monotheistic, sky-father psychoanalytic theories (Rowland, 2017).

The myth of the goddess surfaces in unlikely avatars in the modern world. When political insurgencies and peasant revolts spread in the forest and

FIGURE 4.1 Clay Goddess.

Source: Quratulain, CC BY-SA 3.0, via Wikimedia Commons, https://commons.wikimedia.org/wiki/File:Picture_of_original_Godess.jpg

mining belts of eastern India, an unusual saga unfolds. Dopdi Mejhen is a fugitive – young, passionate, faithful to a cause. The law-enforcers are scouring the land, as rumor has it that she has instigated the murder of an upper-caste landowner, who had stopped farm-workers from drinking water at his well on a blistering summer day. Dopdi and her husband Dulna are landless labourers. They move between villages scouting for work, earning wages from whatever their employers dole out. When drought worsens, and the indignities and atrocities of landlords can be borne no more, farm-workers turn militant. Chaos follows, till local police arrive, capture rebels and haul them into jails. Combing the forests vigorously this time, the police chance upon Dulna, a suspected insurgent, who they quickly gun down. The elderly police chief Senanayak thinks that the dead body could be a bait to lure other rebels. The corpse is left out in the open, but deleye, no one comes to claim Dulna's body. A notice is then issued – Dopdi Mejhen, twenty-seven, wanted, dead or alive.

Dopdi scurries through the countryside hoping to gather food, or information about her group members, some of whom have turned informers. She tries to gauge the extent of her danger, recalling her leader's words about remaining undercover. The police chief Senanayak is supposedly Marxist. But the fact is, he does not care about the plight of landless laborers. Senanayak is determined to capture rebels, and for women like Dopdi, there are special 'encounters'. Dopdi senses danger as she walks through the fields. When her name is called out in the marketplace, she does not turn back. Instead, she makes a hurried detour through the rocks to reach the safety of the forests, but things happen quickly thereafter. Betrayed by her former friends, Dopdi is apprehended. It is a damned end.

Senanayak's cold words 'make her' concludes the seize. Days later, her body ravaged, bruised, searing with pain from the assaults of men in the police camp, Dopdi lay motionless on the ground, barely conscious. But when her name is called out, she picks herself up, and asks where she would have to go. There would be interrogations, more torture, a forced confession even. She vowed to bite off her tongue when that happened. A strip of cloth hung over her bare body. It slithers now as she rises, and she pauses briefly. Then she tears the cloth with her teeth, throws it away and walks forward, ignoring the gaze of the policemen around. When Senanayak enters the courtyard, a volley of sounds greet him – shrill, incoherent, primal. The police chief is unprepared for the scene unfolding before him – a naked woman prisoner, spewing tirade. When Dopdi utters the word 'counter', it occurs to Senanayak that police training manuals had not prepared him for unarmed encounters like this. Or warned him about insurgents like Dopdi. Senanayak calls for his personnel, but Dopdi stands before him laughing, refusing to cover her body, telling him to use her as he wills.

Dopdi's fiery narrative was penned by Marxist-feminist writer Mahasweta Devi (1926–2016), who spent a lifetime working among indigenous communities of India. The title of her story 'Draupadi', is a take on an ancient Indian character named Draupadi from the epic Mahabharata, that suggests feminine rage and revenge, which Mahasweta metaphorized in stories of peasant insurgence. The female body is an object of domination, inscribed with feelings of shame and fear. Dopdi breaks this convention when she ignores the collective gaze on her, and refuses to cover herself. Feminist theoretician Judith Butler writes that the female body is a site of cultural inscription, constantly under siege, on the verge of disruption, and prone to subversive acts (Butler, 2014, pp. 163–168).

Living on the margins of society, divested of power, facing constant threat to life, Dopdi's vulnerability is the site of a primal awakening. Senanayak is barely familiar with its nuances. His uneasiness on seeing her naked is because he realizes that with her, he has stepped into an unfamiliar battleground, where conventional methods of combat would not be effective. Dopdi's subversiveness is a primal form of protest, emanating from her body, instinctual and inborn. Defying notions of shame and fear, she turns her body into an instrument of insurgence. Her refusal to be clothed (which she knows will be used to cover and strip her alternately), and her shrill ululations, are bodily acts that the power hierarchies around her. Postcolonial feminist scholar Gayatri Chakravorty Spivak describes Mahasweta as an intervention journalist, who worked among tribal communities lifelong, compiling oral histories, and documenting class and gender inequities of landless and oppressed people (Spivak, 1997). Mahasweta described her work as liberational. 'I wanted to do it. I had to set myself free and I did not want to listen to anyone. I did what I wanted to … These are things I have to write about and I can't stop' (Sethi, 2012, p. 78). In Dopdi, Mahasweta located a metaphor of feminine emergence, her own even, through disruption of social convention.

Dopdi's connection to her ancestors, to the land, her insurgent activities, protest and anger, are biophilic traits, that shape her agency and mind. In 'Anger in the Body', Naomi R. Goldenberg writes how anger as an emotion is denoted as evil, and displaced on real women, while the notion of a disembodied and puritanized feminine spirit is lauded in religion and culture. Goldenberg says that Melanie Klein proposed that anger is a legitimate emotion that infants demonstrate towards parents, free expression of which allows mature emotions of love and compassion to develop (Goldenberg, 1986). In 'Female Madness and the Feminine Monstrous', Natasa Polgar writes how cultural conception of madness is closely aligned with the notion of the monstrous and the feminine (Polgar, 2021). Female anger denoted as madness is common in psychiatry. But Dopdi's outburst exposes the power asymmetries of her world. It springs from deep within her, in indigenous metaphors that are incoherent to the outside world. Polgar writes how women patients recounted being 'possessed' by a foreign force when they were besieged by feelings of anger, after which they were hospitalized, because it was thought that the Devil had taken possession. Anger is not uncommon in animus constellations, but how is this anger viewed? In Phoolan's narrative, she recalled that her rage was seen by village-folk as strange and uncanny. Dopdi's anger is not alien to her – they are sounds and acts that are absorbed from her ancestral land, and evoked from within her chthonic self, but to Senanayak, they were incoherent.

Female rage threatens not just others, but women as well. While feminist therapists believe that anger could be a legitimate response to socio-cultural imbalances, women themselves are frightened of it, internalizing its negativity and turning it inwards, letting its energies dissipate into guilt, depression, shame and somatic disorders (Mueller and Leidig, 1976). Female emotionalism is associated with love and compassion, or characterized negatively, as irrational thinking. Like the female body that is thrown out of religion because of its erotic nuances, feminine rage is deemed monstrous, nonhuman and unnatural. Female anger is viewed as impure and unholy, and compared to the Devil. Polgar, who evaluates anger from socially and culturally constructed categories, states that anger is, '... ..in part also the history of the clash of cultures between the male, rational and scientific and the feminine, irrational, and vernacular' (Polgar, 2021, p. 71).

Dopdi's story, as also Durga's, are instances of feminine ascendence in chaos and despair. Anger is an aspect of human emotionality, that is in relation to all other emotions. The Indian *Navarasas* denote anger as one of the nine emotions, commonly symbolized in the fury and emotionalism of Shiva, Durga, Kali. Dopdi's anger is, not to be conflated with her indigeneity. In 'Debunking the Myth of "Angry Black Women"' J. Celeste Walley-Jean says how certain stereotypes about black women are perpetuated, where gender and racial issues are made to interact, to project emotions of racial aggression (Walley-Jean, 2009). While anger cannot be stereotyped with indigenousness, it is pertinent to note that anger as a natural emotion that can have appropriate, adaptive and purposeful expression, is rarely valued in therapy or analytic discourse. The ascendant feminine principle in the myth of Durga is also envisioned around anger. It is distinct from the aggression of the gods who are fighting the demons. While their endless warring and combat have produced a cosmic imbalance, Durga's rage has a contextual ground, and is enacted purposefully.

Mahasweta's Dopdi amplifies a subaltern feminine idiom that intersects class, human rights and gender. In Dopdi's many-layered oppression in the hands of rich landowners, rapist police, is a sense of agency that is subversive, primordial, prior to the 'Law of the Father'. An autochthonic tenor marks Mahasweta's writings as if the stories birthed from her womb. The body is often the site of revival, after its destruction. It was the body where Dopdi sensed her rage first when she heard her name summoned by the police; it was the body she used as a weapon against Senanayak. The place of her dismembering and wounding is also the place of her re-emergence. It was a female body, of Draupadi, disrobed by the Kaurava prince Dushasana in the epic Mahabharata, where a beastly revenge was conceived. Draupadi had declared that she would not tie her hair till it was washed with her assaulter's blood. It is the body, crafted as Durga, in the myth of the goddess, that feminine combat skills are witnessed. Its emergence is sporadic, but its constituents are perennial, like the riverbed soil from which the goddess is molded cyclically. The myth of the goddess is embedded in old and new stories, in metaphors of destruction and revival. While Dopdi's eerie chortle signified a bodily defiance, we note also that her fearlessness was nurtured alongside men like Dulna. The other is intimately woven into the feminine. The vivifying relation with the other, of any gender, is fundamental to contra-sexual formations of the self.

Dionysian Reversals and Radical Diversities in the Feminine

In 'Dionysius Reborn in Psychology and Literature', Susan Rowland tells how literature and psychology began as separate disciplines, contesting science and social sciences, each claiming autonomy from the other (Rowland, 2017). Sidestepping psyche in literary narratives, and separating social sciences from literature, because aesthetic and psychological expressions do not converge, warrants a Dionysian reversal in our approach to reading narratives.

The notion of transgenderism in heteropatriarchal worlds has emerged as a prominent idiom in cinematic narratives in India. Cinema has a wide reach in India, capturing collective imagination and engendering conversations through storytelling, image and sound. In the Indian film anthology *Ajeeb Dastaan* (2021), the story of *Geeli Poochie* (Wet Kisses) portrays the complex interface of caste, sexuality and patriarchy, in the story of two lesbian women, a Dalit and a Brahmin.[4] The protagonist Bharti, a Dalit, is a machine operator in a small-town factory, although she qualifies as an accountant. Plush, desk jobs are not for Dalit girls, she is told, when she tries to get an accountant's job in the factory. Settling down into a menial routine at the factory, Bharti learns to ignore the jibes of her male co-workers, who comment on her butch looks. Bharti is aware of her social and gender identity and pines for her lover in private, but she agonizes as much, over her dim life prospects in a caste-ridden, industrial world, which she now inhabits.

When Priya, a pretty young upper-caste girl, takes on the job of an accountant at the office, and befriends her, Bharti's feelings towards her swing between hostility and fondness. Finding that they desire each other is no consolation, for Bharti learns soon enough, that Priya is entrenched in casteist sentiments of her own. The turnaround for Bharti in discovering this is radical. When a confused and conflicted Priya seeks Bharti's advice about her marriage, the latter advises her to have a child, and induce some normalcy into her married life. She offers her house, where Priya and her husband meet up, away from their large extended family. When Priya becomes pregnant and has to take leave from office, Bharti takes over her work. The child's birth brings no joy for Priya, and as she contemplates returning to office, she asks if Bharti would consider being a nanny to her new-born. Bharti asks her to take a break from office instead. With no prospects of Priya's return, the manager asks Bharati's to step into Priya's role. The fleeting triumph in Bharti's eyes as she makes this transition, claiming what she had aspired for herself, is striking. While Priya's dejection about her life becomes more and more apparent, Bharti's steely demeanor hides a quiet jubilation. In a haunting last scene, she sits with Priya sipping tea from a cup that has been specially set aside for her, because as a Dalit she is not allowed to have a tea-cup like others in the household – a scathing reminder of the practice of untouchability in modern-day India. Casteism impairs a romance, even as it impels Bharti forward in a malaise-ridden, bigoted, patriarchal world. The radical ambivalence of the psyche and its gendered alterity is captured in fluid and liminal ways through a series of moving images and sounds, conveying the complexity of lived contexts. Bharti and Priya's affinity in gendered sameness is fragmented by caste, class and privilege, charting very distinct trajectories for each.

Geeli Poochie (Wet Kisses) is not India's first film on queer relations. Issues of transgenderism and homosexuality have been in public discourse since the 1990s. India's first mainstream lesbian film *Fire* was surrounded by controversy on its release. A landmark Supreme Court judgment two decades later in 2018 on Article 377 decriminalized homosexual relations. In fluid and changing dynamics of gender, race, religion, caste and class, the phenomenon of transgenderism is an added nuance. Avgi Saketopoulou writes,

> Trans is a still-evolving term. Currently, it describes a heterogeneous set of individuals who share a felt sense of misalignment between experienced gender and the gender to which they were assigned at birth on the basis of observed sex. Trans includes, at least, the following: people experiencing varying degrees of distress about bodily morphology that marks, or is seen as marking, gender; a subset seeking hormonal interventions to modify secondary sexual characteristics; a group feeling the need to surgically align their body with their self-identified gender; individuals only altering social signifiers (e.g. name, pronouns) but uninterested in medical/surgical procedures; some who experience no bodily distress; and persons who do not identify as male/female, yielding new terms such as "gender non-binary" and "agender" and they/them pronouns.
>
> (Saketopoulou, 2020, p. 1020)

Geeli Poochie portrays, not emotional and bodily ambivalences of transitional states, but an intrapsychic realm, where class and caste intersect gender alterities. The individual negotiates selfhood in competing realms of sexuality, caste and patriarchy. Bharti's feelings of rage at being derogated and discriminated as a Dalit, is shown as more important, than her sexual orientation. When she prioritizes her career aspirations, maneuvers to take on Priya's role, it is a comment on the complexity of her lived world, and the ambivalence and uncertainty of herself, constantly under siege.

Cinematic narratives offer transdisciplinary spaces, through image, story and aesthetic formulations. Luke Hockley writes that 'What we experience in the cinema is an awakening of personal and collective psychological material, which mirrors the way in which images behave in the psyche' (Hockley, 2005, p. 48). While Dopdi's rape and brutality can be imagined in battle zones and war camps anywhere, Bharti's subalternity is particular to the subcontinent, because of its caste nuances. Caste is a phenomenon of psychological and social othering, in which undesirable parts of oneself are projected onto people of different color, race, economic and social status. Its roots are old, and its history is not very unlike racism, colonialism or misogyny. The contents of Vedic religion show many forms of discrimination, as do many other religions of the world. Bharti's ability to not let collective attitudes subvert her sense of self is a sign of feminine thinking and agency, that is unlike descriptions of feminine given by Jung, as characterized by Eros and feeling. Priya, on the other hand, shows neither clear thinking nor relationality. The dialectical tension between the two characters triggers new developments in the story, in Bharti's subversive and affirmative acts of selfhood and independence.

Narratives of psyche implicate social and political realities, as much as they embody the personal. Consciousness is an amalgam of inner and outer. In *Translate this Darkness*, Jungian analyst Claire Douglas describes Christiana Morgan's (1897–1967) childhood, where her mother often tried to rein in an insubordinate daughter (Douglas, 1997). Driven by internalized pressures to conform to collective social standards, Morgan's mother felt compelled to lock Christina inside closets or send her away, when the child acted difficult. In an opulent, seemingly liberal Boston environment, infused with upper-crust privileges, Christiana felt alienated from her ilk, especially the womenfolk, and grappled with an inner darkness. Pining for a fuller relation with her father only intensified her loneliness, as he was unavailable. Her search for self-expression, remained torn between outer adventures and inner creativity, worlds that were never fully reconciled. More than a hundred years later, Susan E Schwartz's *The Absent Father Effect on Daughters* (Schwartz, 2020), tells us how father absences and mother wounds mark the feminine psyche, translating into darknesses of varying kinds, stripping the individual of feeling and connectedness, self-belief and reflexivity.

Jung named the unconscious feminine in men as anima, and denoted feminine inner and masculine outer as being in compensatory relationship with each other. The anima is a soul-image produced in the unconscious of man. It is an inner attitude that finds its outer representation in persons with corresponding qualities (Jung, vol 6, para 808). The notion of a muted, inner feminine is movingly portrayed in the Indian cult film *Udaan* (Flight). When a quiet, demure Rohan is expelled from school and comes to live with his estranged father, he is ill-prepared for what unfolds. An abusive and alcoholic Bhairav Singh is a man Rohan barely imagines as his father. With him is an eight-year-old boy, his son from another marriage. Rohan is mean to his half-brother, but despite their mutual animosity the two are bound by their shared predicaments, in their isolated and uprooted life with Bhairav. The boys are forbidden to address Bhairav as 'father' and are forced to follow his iron-handed discipline. Mocked by Bhairav for his sensitive demeanor and unconventional life-aspirations, Rohan's life in a quaint, suburban town, with a hostile and uncaring Bhairav, is bleak and dismal.

Still, Rohan's affective core radiates an affability, unspoilt by the vicissitudes of life. A glaring absence of women characters in the narrative accentuates Bhairav's dark and turbulent masculinity, and highlights the absent feminine. Its presence is in Rohan's delicate sensibilities and calm demeanour. Memories of his deceased mother and friendship with his uncle, help him navigate an unstable world. But, one day, when he sees his half-brother Arjun hospitalized because of Bhairav's beating, he hits a new low. Nursing the young boy, Rohan realizes the extent of Arjun's helplessness in this mortal hellhole. As he tends to him and bonds with him newly, he ponders over their fate. When Bhairav returns from a business tour and attacks Rohan over his exam results, things come to a climactic end. A violent confrontation, a night spent away from home and a conversation with his uncle, help Rohan decide his future. The boys set off for a faraway city, hoping to build a new life, where they would not be hounded by their father's brutality and heartlessness.

In the film's cathartic final act, Rohan finds his voice, from the firm tenderness of his core and the trials and torments of a difficult adolescence. It is not the narcissism of youth that goads him on this new adventure, but an agency where he is able to think about the future – his own and Arjun's. Rohan's coming-of-age story blends steely firmness with compassion, and a sense of Self that includes the other. Bhairav's disconnect with his sons is not just a reflection of failed attachment relations, but cultural attitudes as well, that keep the masculine isolated from feeling and relationality. His lack of empathy has deep roots in his own childhood, where a secure infant-mother bonding, and an empathetic link with the feminine were not established. Rohan, on the other hand has experienced affective bonding with his mother, evident in the film's brief montages. Despite the trouble and instability of his everyday life, Rohan's link to his compassionate inner core is intact. It is a sharp contrast to Bhairav's, and accentuates the paradoxical nature of their relation. An inner feminine triggers Rohan's transition into adulthood. The notion of Self that we are left with, resonates with Louis Zinkin's concept of Self, that is shaped out of continuous interaction with the other, formed from the environment in which a person lives, inhering neither in personal nor in collective and archetypal, but in an interactive realm between the two (Zinkin, 2008).

In 'Historicizing Anger', Dorothée Sturkenboom writes about the history of emotions in men and women in Dutch culture, showing how the polarization of sexes resulted in the polarization of emotions – superior masculinity does not demonstrate feelings of compassion, and feeling men are viewed as effeminate (Sturkenboom, 2000). Bhairav's hypermasculinity and Rohan's feminized self, are two poles of a contra-sexual dyad. Men and masculine are identified with logos and dominance, while feminine is 'construed as matter, body, unreason, unconsciousness, negativity and sexuality' (Rowland, 2017 p. 21). While these are dominant gender perceptions, Rohan, Dopdi, Bharti, evoke feminine–masculine dualities that are fluid and interchangeable. Judith Butler says that patriarchy has no universal signifier, nor femininity of a particular sex (Butler, 2014). Dopdi, Bharti, Rohan's contra-sexual psyche is dynamic and evolving. The Self is formed from particulars of a lived context, from the body, from disruption and difference with the collective, and from specificities of personal psyche. In comparison, Jung's views about feminine and masculine were stipulative and imbued with hierarchical notions of gender.

'One of the most significant implications of the lively praxial phenomenon is that it implicitly ("unconsciously") embodies the reflective practice of living on along with the completely other, radically different, with the wholly unlikely', writes Venkat Rao about heterogeneous cultural formations that counter linear, universalist, hegemonic theories of knowledge (Rao, 2018, p. 8). The animus or anima become problematic when described hegemonically, with fixed and one-sided characterization of the archetype. A Dionysian reordering of psyche in fluid and intersecting realms of psychological and social is needed. Susan Rowland writes about trans-disciplinarity that is non-unifying, that helps loosen boundaries between disciplines without losing specific ontologies (Rowland, 2017). Such an approach carries the multiplicity of lived worlds instead of preconceived unities, where narratives disrupt rigid and formalized boundaries and challenge one-sidedness. A Dionysian reversal of forces marks the feminine-masculine dyad in the stories of Durga, Dopdi, Bharti and Rohan. The dead rise, voices emerge and the self is resurrected from loss, pain and longing, in psyche's radical interaction and engagement with the other.

Notes

1 Consider, for instance, the journeys and cross-cultural explorations of Fa-Hien, Hiuen Tsang, Al Biruni and others who came to India to inquire about ancient Indian literature from the beginning of common era.
2 The Hindu Vedic calendar is a lunisolar almanac called *panjika* used for marking auspicious days of worship, festivals and crop calendars, different from the Gregorian calendar.
3 See UNESCO, 'Durga Puja inscribed on the UNESCO Representative List of the Intangible Cultural Heritage of Humanity', Press Release, 15 December 2021, Available at https://en.unesco.org/news/durga-puja-inscribed-unesco-representative-list-intangible-cultural-heritage-humanity.
4 Brahmin is the highest caste in the hegemonic caste system of India. They are priestly members among Hindus who officiate religious ceremonies and rituals, follow ancient Vedic texts, and follow coded customs and traditions. In contemporary society, their influence is not much, although the conservative Brahmins follow endogamic and other social practices till today. Dalit is a disenfranchised caste, also known as untouchables.

References

Banerji, C. (2006) *Hour of the Goddess: Memories of Women, Food and Ritual in Bengal*. New Delhi: Penguin India.

Bhattacharji, S. (1995) *Legends of Devi*. Kolkata: Orient Blackswan.

Bishop, P. (2012) 'The Archaic: Timeliness and Timelessness', in Bishop, P. (ed.), *The Archaic: The Past in the Present*. Hove, East Sussex: Routledge, pp. 226–247.

Butler, J. (2014) *Gender Trouble: Feminism and the Subversion of Identity*. New York: Routledge.

Coward, H. (1985) *Jung and Eastern Thought*. SUNY Series in Transpersonal and Humanistic Psychology. Albany, NY: SUNY Press.

Douglas, C. (1997) *Translate This Darkness: The Life of Christiana Morgan*. Princeton, NJ: Princeton University Press.

Ellenberger, H. F. (1981) *The Discovery of The Unconscious: The History and Evolution of Dynamic Psychiatry*. New York: Basic Books.

Elliott, A. and Prager, J. (eds.) (2016) *The Routledge Handbook of Psychoanalysis in the Social Sciences and Humanities*. London: Routledge.

Freud, S. (1913, 2001) *Totem and Taboo*. London: Routledge.

Freud, S. (1939) *Moses and Monotheism*, translated from the German by Katherine Jones. London: Hogarth Press.

Giegerich, W. (2012) *What is Soul?* New Orleans, LA: Spring Journal Books.

Goldenberg, N. R. (1986) 'Anger in the Body: Feminism, Religion and Kleinian Psychoanalytic Theory', *Journal of Feminist Studies in Religion*, 2(2), pp. 39–49.

Hockley, L. (2005) 'Cinema as Illusion and Reality', Spring: *Journal of Archetype and Culture*, 73, pp. 41–53.

Jung, C. G. 1969. 'Archetypes of the Collective Unconscious', in *The Archetypes and the Collective Unconscious*, Vol. 9, pt. 1, The Collected Works of C. G. Jung. Princeton, NJ: Princeton University Press.

Jung, C. G. (1970) 'What India Can Teach Us', in *Civilization in Transition*, Vol. 10, The Collected Works of C. G. Jung. Princeton, NJ: Princeton University Press.

Jung C. G. (2018) *History of Modern Psychology: Lectures Delivered at the ETH Zurich 1933-1934* in Shamdasani, S. (ed.). Princeton, NJ: Princeton University Press.

Kakar, S. (2003) *Culture and Psyche*. New Delhi: Oxford University Press.

Khan, M. S. (1976) 'al-Bīrūnī and the Political History of India', *Oriens*, 25/26, pp. 86–115, https://www.jstor.org/stable/1580658.

Mishra, J. S. (1979) 'A New Light on Albiruni's Travel in India', *Proceedings of the Indian History Congress*, 40, pp. 80–82.

Mueller, K. and Leidig, M. W. (1976) 'Women's Anger and Feminist Therapy', *Frontiers: A Journal of Women Studies*, 1(3), pp. 23–30.

Mueller, M. (1882) *India: What Can It Teach Us?*, A Course of Lectures Delivered before the University of Cambridge, https://www.gutenberg.org/files/20847/20847-h/20847-h.htm.

Mueller, M. (2007) 'On the Truthful Character of the Hindus', Lecture 2, in *India: What Can It Teach Us?*, https://www.gutenberg.org/files/20847/20847-h/20847-h.htm#LECTURE_I.

Nandy, A. (2021) 'Psychoanalytic Sociology and Post-Colonial Predicament: An Interview by Livio Boni' in Nandy, A. and Saccidanandan (eds.), *Breakfast with Evil and Other Risky Ventures*. New Delhi: Oxford University Press, pp. 229–244.

Nandy, A. and Darby, P. (2018) 'Challenging the Ruling Paradigms of the Global Knowledge System: Ashis Nandy in Conversation with Phillip Darby', *Postcolonial Studies*, 21(3), pp. 278–284.

Polgar, N. (2021) 'Female Madness and the Feminine Monstrous: Genre as Confinement and Genre as Affective Repository', *Narrative Culture*, 8(1), pp. 58–81.

Rao, D. V. (ed.). (2018) *Critical Humanities from India: Contexts, Issues, Futures*. London: Routledge.

Rowland, S. (2017) *Remembering Dionysus: Revisioning Psychology and Literature in C.G. Jung and James Hillman*. London: Routledge.

Saketopoulou, A. (2020) 'Thinking Psychoanalytically, Thinking Better: Reflections on Transgender', *The International Journal of Psychoanalysis*, 101(5), pp. 1019–1030.

Segal, R. (2004) *Myth: A Very Short Introduction*. New York: Oxford University Press.

Sen, A. (2001) 'History and the Enterprise of Knowledge', *Social Scientist*, 29(1/2), pp. 3–15.

Sengupta, S. (2022) 'Katabasis in and Indian Myth: Savitri Encounters Yama', in Bishop, P., Dawson, T., and Gardner, L. (eds.), *The Descent of the Soul and the Archaic: Katabasis and Depth Psychology*. London: Routledge, pp. 117–132.

Shamdasani, S. (2003) *Jung and the Making of Modern Psychology: The Dream of a Science*. Cambridge, UK: Cambridge University Press.

Smadja, E. (2015) *Freud and Culture*. London: Routledge.

Spivak, G. C. (trans.) (1997) 'Introduction', *Breast Stories* by Mahasweta Devi. Kolkata: Seagull Books.

Schwartz, S. E. (2020) *The Absent Father Effect on Daughters: Father Desire, Father Wounds*. London: Routledge.

Sethi, S. (2012) *The Big Bookshelf: Sunil Sethi in Conversation with 30 Famous Writers*. New Delhi: Penguin Books.

Sturkenboom, D. (2000) 'Historicizing the Gender of Emotions: Changing Perceptions in Dutch Enlightenment Thought', *Journal of Social History*, 34(1), pp. 55–75.

Tagore, R. (1921) 'The Union of Cultures' *The Modern Review*, 30(5), https://en. wikisource.org/wiki/Works_of_Tagore_from_the_Modern_Review,_1909-24/ The_Union_of_Cultures.

Walley-Jean, J. C. (2009) 'Debunking the Myth of the "Angry Black Woman": An Exploration of Anger in Young African American Women', *Black Women, Gender + Families*, 3(2), pp. 68–86.

Zinkin, L. (2008) 'Your Self: Did You Find It or Did You Make It?' *Journal of Analytical Psychology*, 53, pp. 389–406.

5

SYNCHRONICITY

Synchronicity and Jung

The appearance of the term *animus* in a dream image, recounted in chapter 2, calls for an inquiry into the phenomenon of synchronicity, or meaningful coincidence of unrelated objects. Jung invented the term synchronicity, defining it as acausal links that erupt spontaneously and bring unrelated entities together in meaningful ways. In a letter to Carl Jung in 1949, Austrian physicist Wolfgang Pauli drew his attention to Arthur Schopenhauer's essay titled 'The Apparent Design in the Fate of the Individual' (Meier, 2001, p. 37). Schopenhauer had reflected on causally disconnected phenomena, or chance events, where necessity and chance direct an individual's fate (Schopenhauer, 1913). Historian of science Susan Geiser writes, 'Here Schopenhauer develops the idea of an ultimate union of necessity and chance, which reveals itself to us as a '… ›force‹, ›which links together all things, even those that are causally unconnected, and does it in such a way that they come together just at the right moment' (Geiser, 2005, p. 288). Geiser notes that Leibniz too assumed a fundamental link between all elements of existence. These elements or monads are parallel to each other, but do not share reciprocal relations. In his letter, Pauli mentioned that Schopenhauer's idea was a precursor to Jung's notion of synchronicity. On his insistence that Jung be more precise about the term 'acausal', Jung defined synchronicity as an ordering of events in inner and outer worlds without any apparent cause (Meier, 2001, p. 60).

For Jung, acausality was a defining feature of synchronicity (Meier, 2001, p. 68). The western notion of time as cause and effect compared to the eastern concept of time as simultaneous, had been noted in his seminar on Dream Analysis in 1928 (Jung, 1984). He had used the term *synchronism*

DOI: 10.4324/9780429423727-5

then (Jung, 1984). Later he differentiated it from synchronicity, which he used for the first time at Richard Wilhelm's memorial address of 1930. He said that he was using the concept of synchronicity for a special kind of coincidence of two or more causally unrelated events, that is distinct from synchronism or a simultaneous occurrence of two events (Jung, 1969b, para. 849). He remarked that discussions with Einstein and Richard Wilhelm had led him to think about acausal phenomena (Geiser, 2005, p. 277). But it was Pauli whom Jung acknowledged as having given him courage to pursue the topic (Enz, 2010, p. 428).

The notion of meaningfulness in chance coincidences was intriguing for Pauli. Jung emphasized that synchronistic events triggered a widening of consciousness, or transition from unstable psychic state to stable consciousness. As they discussed, the uniting of opposites seemed to Pauli to be directed by a higher force. It was similar to the concept of complementarity in quantum theory (Atmanspacher and Fuchs, 2014). Jung called this the principle of *unus mundus,* or a unifying reality underlying all multiplicity. Pauli and Jung corresponded over two decades (1932–1957) on 'the psychophysical problem' or the interface between physical and mental, as Swiss physicist Harald Atmanspacher describes in *The Pauli-Jung Conjecture and Its Impact Today* (Atmanspacher and Fuchs, 2014, Intro). Jung's lectures at Bailey Island on Pauli's dreams, titled *Dream Symbols of the Individuation Process* were delivered in New York in 1936–1937 (Geiser, 2019). While both deliberated on how matter and psyche could be related, Jung's spiritualizing of the notion of archetype and the psyche as a conscious-unconscious whole, were challenging propositions for Pauli. The latter wanted to give importance to matter in relation to psyche. (Mind-matter relationship has been discussed as dual aspect monism by Cambray and Atmanspacher in recent times). Even though Pauli looked for a unified science that integrates psyche and matter, scientific thinking and intuitive feeling, Kepler and Fludd, finding a language that holds these dualities and accommodates the irrational, was not easy (Geiser, 2005 p. 218). Nonetheless, it was Pauli's involvement with the topic that helped Jung foreground synchronicity, and propose a theory about acausal connections and the unconscious. Also, it was Pauli who helped Jung note the psychoid properties of the archetype.

Webbed Fields

Pauli was not unfamiliar with India. He had visited India in 1952–1953, on invitation from Indian nuclear physicist Homi J. Bhabha, whom he had met in Zurich and Geneva, in 1939. Bhabha had referred to Pauli's work in his research at Cambridge (Enz, 2010, p. 352). In mid 1930s, Homi Jehangir Bhabha (1909–1966) was at Cambridge on an Isaac Newton fellowship pursuing his doctoral studies on cosmic radiation, when he met Niels Bohr, and began apprenticing under him. Pauli and Bhabha's encounter some years later, was not unexpected, given their shared scientific interests, and Pauli's proximity to Bohr. Pauli also met Indian Nobel laureate C.V. Raman (known for his work on light scattering); both attended the Lindau Nobel Laureate meeting in 1956 in Germany. In November 1952, Pauli visited India, with his wife Franca. 'India is a strange country of the most extreme contrasts, from the most beautiful temples (on the island of Elephanta they are magnificent) to mass misery, from airplanes to serpents and vultures, from palms with coconuts to bacterias. My wife got sick by it (now she slowly recovers) and I was enormously stimulated and "cranked" (*angekurbelt*). Thus India has produced a pair of opposites with my wife and myself'. And later he comments: 'And, anyway, I must reject the whole tendency of spiritualization which is hostile towards matter' (Enz, 2010, p. 473).

India had constellated various kinds of opposites in Jung's journey too. His links with India were formed from unknown sources, whose implications were not just in the personal. Pauli thought that archetypes should not be viewed merely as psychic phenomena. This made Jung consider psychoid properties of archetypes (Geiser, 2005, p. 346). Both agreed that archetypes signify transitional psychic states. Transitional states, or psyche's movement from diffused states of consciousness to complex self-organizing systems, have been explored in post-Jungian discourse in recent times (Skar, 2004; Hogenson, 2005; Cambray, 2006). The notion of unifying psychoid is of particular relevance when we look at synchronicity across cultures, or the spontaneous ways in which unrelated realms become connected, for instance, Jung's links with India. Synchronicities reveal how seemingly unrelated entities converge, like the dream image of the book of which I had no foreknowledge. It suggests what Pauli had observed too – archetypes contain elements that go beyond the personal psyche.

Pertinent to mention, that Jung's notion of unconscious and Indian concept of consciousness belonged to vastly different intellectual traditions. Yet, the two sides were in interaction, and the distant worlds of east and west often converged. The period when Jung was probing into the Upanishads and the Kundalini texts in early 1900s, eastern spiritual philosophy was in wide circulation in the west. Upsurge of interest in Indian spiritual traditions meant not just exchange of religious ideas, but translation of Sanskrit and Pali texts, and numerous cross-cultural explorations. Journeys by Herman Hesse, Alice Boner, Stella Kramrisch, Romain Roland, Heinrich Zimmer and many others, are among them. Austrian-born, Indological scholar Kramrisch (1896–1993) conducted pioneering research on Indian theogony during her Indian sojourn, and also taught at Tagore's university, Visva-Bharathi in Shantiniketan. Later, a similar Indological exploration was conducted by Wendy Doniger, as a student at Shantiniketan. John Woodroffe's

(1865–1936) tenure in British India included study of Tantric texts, translation of *sat-chakra-nirupana* and Jung procuring Woodroffe's book (Sengupta, 2013). Tagore's world tours, and Hermann Keyserling's and Olga Fröbe-Kapteyn's east-west forums, kept east and west in dialogue in the decade of twenties and thirties.

Jung had met Hermann Keyserling through Oskar Schmidt, author of *Psychoanalyse and Yoga*. Keyserling was known to Rabindranath Tagore, and to Argentinian writer Victoria Ocampo. Tagore had met Ocampo during his world tour of 1930 – the latter had read Andre Gide's translation of Gitanjali, and had invited him to Argentina. Jung on the other hand knew Keyserling well, and had met Ocampo in Zurich (McGuire and Hull, 1977, p. 82). Ocampo, Keyserling, Tagore and Jung's weblike links spanned three continents and reflected the highly charged field of east-west relations of early twentieth century. Further still, Jung met Vedanta spiritualists Boshi and Gertrude Sen, Swami Yatisarnanada in the same decade, and German sinologist Ervin Rousselle, Pali scholar C. Rhys Davids, French orientalist Paul Masson-Oursel, Mircea Eliade and others, at Eranos gatherings.

It was not only how spontaneously these links emerged, but the curious contents of some of their histories. A glimpse of oriental scholar Rhys Davids' life reveals some of it. Colchester-born, Welsh philologist, T.W. Rhys Davids (1843–1922), was initiated into in Pali studies during his posting in Ceylon under British administrative services. Retrieving Pali transcripts, learning Pali, Sinhala, Tamil and Sanskrit, transcribing archeological inscriptions and writing for the Asiatic Society journal, Rhys Davids, pioneered Buddhist Pali studies in the subcontinent, introducing Pali canon to the western world. His sudden dismissal from colonial services and abrupt departure from the subcontinent put a break to his work, and caused him severe distress. Rhys Davids returned to England, to initiate Pali scholarship in Britain. Like Woodroffe, he tendered himself wholeheartedly to eastern scholarship, and like him, faced several personal adversities on his return home. Lorna S. Devaraja notes, 'His interests centred round Buddhism and the vast field of Pali canonical literature. His wife Caroline Rhys Davids left on record that during this phase of his life, "Rhys Davids was haunted and pursued by the spiritual legacy bequeathed to him from Ceylon' (Dewaraja, 1996, p. 5).

In these complex and mutating histories, interactions were not always synergistic. Dialogues were marked by differences, and personal setbacks were not uncommon. Recall Jung's near-fatal brush with amoebic dysentery in Calcutta, during his 1938 tour in India. When Jung crossed paths with Indian philosopher Surendranath Dasgupta, a Griffith prize awardee, Cambridge scholar, known for his authoritative work on *The History of Indian Philosophy*, the two got along, but their interaction did not yield anything substantial (Guggenbühl, 2008). Jung spent an evening with him at his Calcutta residence and in return hosted him in Zurich in 1939, inviting him for talks at the Psychology Club. Dasgupta was one of the earliest to have elaborated on the six Indian philosophical schools, after Max Mueller's *The Six Systems of Indian Philosophy* (Dasgupta, 1922; Mueller, 1919).

Dasgupta is part of Jung-India history, also on account of his association with Mircea Eliade. As Eliade's first teacher of Sanskrit and yoga philosophy from 1928 to 1930 and his host in Calcutta, Dasgupta and Eliade were well linked, till nineteen-year-old Eliade became involved with Dasgupta's teenage daughter Maitreyi, much to Dasgupta's displeasure. The story of this cross-cultural romance was narrated by Maitreyi Devi, many years later in her award-winning book, *Na Hanyate* (It Does not Die) (Devi, 1994). When the news surfaced, Eliade's tutelage under Dasgupta was aborted. He headed north to seek yoga teachers in the Himalayan region, as yoga tenets were ritually practiced and taught by ascetics living here. David Gordon White writes that Eliade's theories are critiqued today, especially his concept of homo religious and the argument that Indian yoga abolishes the notion of time (Eliade, 2009, pp. xiii–xxvi). Still, Eliade remains one of the foremost western scholars to have studied yoga in India, under an Indian Sanskritist. Eliade met Tagore in Shantiniketan in 1928, through Dasgupta. Much later, he met Jung at Eranos in the 1950s and interviewed him at length (Oldmeadow, 1995). These links highlight how the broader historical field was aligned when Jung's eastern inquiries were in progress. The webbed histories indicate extensive underlying connections between worlds, where specific coincidences emerged.

Acausal Cultural Links

Jung surmised that the East bases much of its science on irregular coincidences and considers it as more reliable than causality. Synchronism is therefore a predisposition of the East, while causality a quality of the West (Jung, 1984).

Jung's meetings with Alice Boner, Alfred Wurfel, W.S. Ratnavale, Inder Sen, Arwind Vasavada, Arindam Basu and Samiran Bannerji were chance events, that had no causal basis (Sengupta, 2013). The historical remnants of these encounters led to my discovery of a cache of archival documents in India pertaining to Jung. It was a chance occurrence, since there are no Jungian institutions and repositories in India. It was the science congress association of Calcutta that had preserved historical records of Jung's visit. Calcutta was the epicenter of India's scientific and political activities, in the decade of the thirties. Jung's journey in 1938 emerged from a surprise invitation from the British government, since Jung had no extant links with the scientific establishment in India or the Indian Psychoanalytic Association. These synchronicities occurred when Jung was inquiring into Indian texts, and suggest transindividual, transcultural elements, in synchronistic phenomena.

In a dream during the initial phase of my Jungian work. I found that I was at a learning retreat on the outskirts of my city. Inside, at the center of the estate, stood a circular enclosure, with a thatched roof and red sandstone floor. The space opened out on all sides, to stretches of green. At the center of the enclosure, on the red floor was a square grey stone, inside which was a fire. It resembled a ritual *yagna* or sacred fire. A wedding rite was being conducted, and a tall, European couple stood behind the fire. They were dressed in pristine white silk. An Indian priest seated before them, recited some hymns as he conducted a wedding. I was dressed in traditional Indian attire, and looked much smaller than the bridal pair. At first, I fetched objects for the ritual and handed them over to the priest; later, I stood aside, and watched the ceremony along with villagers from the neighborhood.

The dream signified a transpersonal field. The wedding couple were European, and had a distant, otherworldly aura around them. The pastoral setting, the ritual fire, the villagers and the priest were a sharp contrast to the couple. They represented a syzygy, and their length and form radiated an ethereality. The muted sheen of their clothes enhanced this ethereal feel. In contrast, the other figures in the dream wore colorful, earthy textiles and appeared smaller. In Indian religion, fire is a uniting symbol between human world and the heavens. The square stone and the circular pavilion (*mandapam*) were aligned in opposition. The dream conveyed an interface between worlds, with the wedding ensemble showing my place in that interface. I was neither being married nor conducting the marriage, but witnessing a rite. I stood at a distance, along with the villagers, whose earthy simplicity and concreteness surrounded me. This was necessary to avert an identification with the archetypal image because the mystical pair and the sacred objects evoked numinous feelings. Without going into details of the nuances of the dream, and the many analytical hours that were needed to metabolize its numinosity and affect, I would like to emphasize the transcultural and transpersonal field that the dream highlighted, and the unrelated worlds that were linked through a synchronistic image.

Harold Atmanspacher's notion of incompatible parts emerging from a whole, and the 'participating observer' who introduces a certain subjectivity into research instead of being a detached scientific observer, may be relevant here (Atmanspacher and Fuchs, 2014, p. 9). I am suggesting, that unrelated entities like Jung and India that have no shared origins, come together through necessity and chance, and through broader historical forces. Discrete entities are connected over expansive timelines and geographies, that implicate not just individual lives, but cultural traditions. Individuals encounter the other, become driven by its force, and find their lives altered. So also, culture. It is an individuating process, which Jung alluded to when he reflected that he was taken out of the Indian world, and reminded that India was not his task, but only a part of his journey, a significant part that would carry him closer to his goal (Jung, 1989, p. 282). Coincidences of culture brought Max Mueller, John Woodroffe (Arthur Avalon), Rhys Davids, and others in contact with India. As Jung himself, whose original dream of a subterranean phallus, has a parallel in the ubiquitous *lingam* of Indian religion.

Roderick Main points out interrelated levels of meaning in synchronicities. A paralleling of two or more events, numinosity and emotional charge, individuation, and archetypal significance (Main, 2014). I would distill them in a similar way:

1 Eruption of dreams and synchronistic events in the personal psyche.
2 An *abaissement du niveau mental*, that aids the emergence of unconscious contents – dreams, visions, prescience, affect, complexes.
3 An *enantiodromia* or compensatory drive to fulfill what is absent or repressed from consciousness.
4 Personal contents align with collective history. Cultural other is fore-grounded in the psyche.
5 Individual lives become oriented towards exploring this. Schopenhauer's will or destiny.
6 More acausal coincidences are triggered between personal and collective worlds, leading to a rupture of old order, psyche's descent and rebirth. Unconscious contents are integrated gradually leading to regeneration of psyche and development of new psychological attitude.
7 A reordering of consciousness through assimilation of incompatible psychic contents.

Cultural Synchronicities

In *Synchronicity: Nature and Psyche in an Interconnected Universe,* Joseph Cambray discusses the notion of cultural synchronicities in history (Cambray, 2009). Cambray writes that it is the 'notion of synchronicity beyond the moment of the initial occurrence of a meaningful coincidence to include extensions of emergent events throughout a protracted period of time, not based on or reducible to simple cause and effect' (Cambray, 2009, p. 106). Here boundaries of subject and object collapse, and a psychoid archetype emerges. Cultural synchronicities have produced war and conquest, as well as creative synergies and discoveries. I have shown in preceding narratives how cultural synchronicities produce new synergies and insights in the field of knowledge. Here is another capsule from history.

Indian mathematician Srinivasa Ramanujan's (1887–1920) seminal encounter and collaboration with British mathematician G.H. Hardy (1877–1947) was a meeting of ancient Indian, intuitive mathematical acumen with modern, rational, western empiricism. Ramanujan, a penurious Brahmin from southern India, untrained in academic methods, showed mathematical prowess from a young age. His conception of numbers came from astrology and archaic mathematical games that his mother taught him in childhood, in an impoverished Brahminical household. It was the Oxbridge mathematician Hardy who read Ramanujan's theorems, that established the latter's fame at Cambridge. Again, it was a chance event – a bunch of mathematical transcripts that Hardy received by post from Ramanujan, which led to the latter's invitation to Cambridge. Ramanujan was at that time a struggling government employee in India living on a paltry salary, working eccentrically on mathematical problems in his free time. In a curious partnership between a British academic and an Indian mathematician, incompatible elements of intuitive, speculative mathematical knowledge were blended with modern, western empirical methods. The two men had nothing in common, but found a partnership that was intellectually productive. Ashis Nandy writes, 'The most remarkable aspect of Ramanujan's encounter with the West was however his relationship with Hardy. Neither of them were the same after meeting the other, ... Hardy gave him exactly what he needed: non-intrusive nurture and "unemotional" support' (Nandy, 1995, p. 117). Much like other cross-cultural pioneers, Ramanujan's life at Cambridge was marked by intense health setbacks, loneliness and eventually, a premature death.

In east-west exchanges, the other has either produced exultation and imitation of the exotic, or violent suppression and denigration. Cultural othering has been a topic of fierce criticism in postcolonial discourse (Nandy, 2009). The Ramanujan-Hardy encounter was different – two discrete scientific minds came together without losing their individual ontologies and created something new. J.W. Clarke writes that, despite his proclivity towards India, Jung was aware of cultural crosscurrents. 'He was acutely aware of the conceptual problems involved in transposing crucial Oriental terms into Western languages, and his recognition of the necessity to maintain the 'otherness' of the writings and cultures he was dealing with has echoes in important current intellectual debates' (Clarke, 1994, p. 26). Jung was more in touch the archaic elements of culture than actual socio-political realities, but even in the archaic and ancient, Jung noted distinctions. What Clarke notes as Jung's interests in alchemy and Gnostic texts as being the cause of his dwindling interests in India, is not entirely true. The following section explains why Jungian and Indian thought can be correlated, only through a qualifying of their differences.

Trajectories of Knowledge

The political and cultural histories of east and west have had very distinct trajectories from the beginning, producing their own unique traditions of knowledge. The earliest known human civilization in the east, the Indus Valley, located on the northwestern border of India, dates back to 2300 BCE. The first known human activity in the region, preceded this settlement by several thousand years. Both Harappa and Mohenjo-daro settlements of the Indus civilization, were urban centers with flourishing agrarian systems and trade practices. Archeological evidence indicates advanced civic consciousness among dwellers, knowledge of art, architecture, symbols and inscriptions and life in planned habitats. In time, these early settlements disintegrated, and a band of Indo-Aryan immigrants, with Sanskrit as their language entered India from Persia and nearby regions. They dominated the local inhabitants, and over the next few centuries went on to establish a culture, that came to be known as the Aryan civilization.

The body of knowledge that was created in this period from around 1000 BCE to fifth or sixth century CE or even later, form early transcripts of knowledge in India, along with an unidentified number of oral transmissions. They contain philosophical treatises, sacred books, mathematical and astronomical writings, ecology, environment, agriculture, politics, medicinal texts, astronomy, grammar, mythology, epics, poetry, as well as actual objects of art, music, architecture, iconography, sculpture, inscriptions, much of which has survived till present time. The notion of India as an ancient entity comes from these historical antecedents. The western world has remained divided about its significance. While German and British orientalists like Max Mueller and William Jones attached inordinate value to these archaic cultural tomes, colonial historians like Thomas Macaulay and James Mill denigrated Indian civilization, citing it as backward, retrograde and primitive.

Vedic literature forms the basis of classical Indian knowledge but it is to noted, that non-textual, indigenous knowledge traditions, have existed alongside literary texts, for centuries. Apart from this, political incursions and cross-cultural sojourns left their own imprints, for instance, Buddhist and Jain religious texts, and Islamic art, aesthetics, music and literature. Hindu religion underwent periods of instability and flux, and attempted various reformist moves, till the colonial era. The point to be noted in this brief outline is that the link with religion or religious symbols remained uninterrupted in India, and influenced the development of knowledge. This is crucial, when compared to the west, where Enlightenment induced a split from orthodox church, and the onset of reason separated religious consciousness from scientific and philosophical knowledge.

The history of unconscious in the west that Jung, Sonu Shamdasani and others have elaborated has its origins in post-Enlightenment scientific rationality – a western legacy, that has no historical parallel in the east (Jung, 2018). The idea of scientific psychology, separate from philosophy, anthropology, theology and metaphysics is a development of late nineteenth-century western science. It had questions like religion and metaphysics perhaps, but aspired to address them through empirical methods. When Swiss philosopher Theodore Flournoy (1854–1920) became the first to be offered a scientific position in psychology, at the University of Geneva in 1892, the discipline of psychology as a science was noticed. American philosopher and psychologist William James, called psychology a hope of science, not a science like physics (Shamdasani, 2003, p. 5). However promising, the problem of too many approaches and methods left the field inundated. By the turn of the century, the domain had proliferated so much, that there was a psychology for every ailment and every unnatural phenomenon. Jung's interest in studying psychology, aligned with the growth of psychology as a discipline in the West. Its emphasis was on empirical inquiry and experimentation rather than speculation, and exploring the scientific veracity of subjective inner world.

A counterapproach to materialist concretist psychology, was German philosopher Wilhelm Dilthey's (1833–1911) notion that psychology was separate from natural sciences – the latter was based on sense-based facts, while the former consisted of inner experiences, and belonged to human sciences. Causal explanation of psychic phenomenon was considered reductionist, while psychic life as having an inner purposive goal was thought to be true. The conflict between experimental method and descriptive approach became part of the discipline's evolution itself. Experimental psychology continued to flourish nonetheless. Jean-Martin Charcot, Alfred Binet and others identified dominant patterns of human behavior, and structured these as typologies. Experiments showed how individual minds are oriented differently – sensory, imaginative, emotional, observational, etc. Understanding individual differences became known as Differential psychology. Parallelly, study of hysteria, somnambulism, seances, gained momentum.

The question of mentalities or typologies was central to early psychology. William James, Alphonse Maeder and Jung offered their own interpretations, with Jung even suggesting cases of hysteria and schizophrenia as examples of extraversion and introversion in individual typologies. He noted that there were differences in 'localizations of libido' similar to what Wilhelm Ostwald categorized as classics and romantics, Wilhelm Worringer termed abstraction and empathy, and Nietzsche defined as Dionysian and Apollonian. It was discussed that Jung's split from Freud was because of typological differences. Jung argued that the empirical psychology he conceived had its history in philosophy, and this was outside the purview of Freud and his followers (Jung, 1961). By 1914, he had differentiated Freud's analytic-reductive method and its causal basis from his constructive-synthetic approach. In Jung's approach, the psyche had a unifying, synthesizing telos (Shamdasani, 2003, p. 81). Through various arguments about typology and personality, the struggle to define psychology as a science continued.

A large part of this work involved dreams, whose significance philosophers like Descartes, Locke and others had attempted to understand earlier. Eighteenth century perception of dreams as waking thought was one view; the German romantic view of dreams as the essence of soul was another. Later, dreams were linked to hallucinations, insanity and unconscious mind. During this time, study of mediums flourished. In Zurich, the publication of Theodore Flournoy's *From India to Planet Mars* (1899), was significant for positioning the notion of unconscious. Swiss psychiatrist Alphonse Maeder argued that dreams were not only expressions of repressed infantile wishes, but conveyed unconscious moral conflicts.

Jung presented the history of unconscious in his lectures of 1933–1934 at ETH, where he cited Kant as being the first to understand that consciousness had a very limited range, and that the realm of unconscious was much larger (Jung, 2018, Lecture 2, p. 13). However, separating the notion of psychological unconscious from metaphysical speculations was not easy. Jung thought that philosophers like Hegel and Schelling, projected the unconscious into metaphysical speculations, especially in ideas about the dark. British empiricists George Berkeley and David Hume tied mental phenomena to the realm of sensations and instinct, but Jung related the unconscious to soul. The soul was traditionally located in religious phenomena, and had become dissociated in modern man. Soul and symbolic life were diminished from an overemphasis on reason, Jung thought. In medieval era, this gap was expressed in the quest for the mysterious and exotic, in journeys to the Orient. The quest for soul, was in Jung's view, the first stirrings of psychology. Jung said that philosophers like Leibnitz, Kant, Hegel, Schelling referred to obscure representations of the mind, or notions of the eternally unconscious, alluding to the soul. Through significant experimentation and observation, the concept of unconscious was located in irrational mental phenomena, dreams, seances, fantasies, hypnosis, around the time when Jung began his psychiatric education. He subsequently conducted his work on dreams, association tests, psychological complexes and typologies.

This brief and incomplete description of the history of unconscious is outlined here to underscore the fact that such an evolution of thought in relation to the psyche and the unconscious, did not occur in the history of knowledge in India. Surendranath Dasgupta notes that the dogmas of karma, rebirth and *moksha* formed primary constituents of early Indian philosophy. It had signifiers such as *gunas, vrittas, manas, citta* and *moksha*. On *moksha* or salvation, Dasgupta wrote that 'Opinions differ in different systems of Hindu philosophy regarding the exact nature of this state, i.e., whether this is an inert state, or a state of pure thoughtless intelligence, or a state of intelligence which is also supreme bliss. But whatever may be these differences, there is general agreement that all systems of Hindu thought have before them the ultimate goal of the absolute, perfect and final freedom of the soul from mind, and all that is mental and physical, and the ultimate cessation of the cycles of rebirth' (Dasgupta, 1941, p. 226). Dasgupta denotes mental phenomenon as *vikalpa*. One of the constituents of vikalpa is false knowledge, which stems from avidya or ignorance. This is the nearest Indian reference to the unconscious, but this is not analogous to the concept of unconscious as made up of instincts, ego, self, persona, shadow, anima, animus, complexes, dissociation, defenses, affect, etc. Avidya, (false knowledge), *asmitā* (egoism), *raga* (attachment), *dvesa* (antipathy), *abhiniveśa* (self-love), are elements linked to *tamas* or darkness. Tamas obstructs consciousness but again, the notion of consciousness here is metaphysical, without reference to psyche. The constituents of Indian psychology are based on speculative ideas. Dasgupta mentions that instincts are a part of personality, but offers no elaborations as to how instincts function within the psyche. 'By personality, I mean here our entire complex structure, including our biological or animal tendencies and cravings, temperament, character, emotions and emotional outlook, will and conduct, in fact, the totality of our interrelated experiences' (Dasgupta, 1941, p. 377).

As evident, the Indian premises have no direct correlation with western empirical psychology, in inquiries into individual seances, dreams, visions, delusions, hallucinations and other mental phenomena. On yoga psychology, Dasgupta states that the essential elements are neutral reals called gunas, whose noumenal nature is unknown. The gunas, express themselves in properties of sattva, rajas, tamas, which are mental states fundamental to all. These are not similar to Jung's psychological types. The gunas range from illumined (sattvic) state of mind, to the dark, inert, tamas. The impassioned rajas falls in between the two. Human personality is characterized by one or the other guna. According to yoga psychology, all mental and physical states rise from gunas, comparable somewhat to Jung's notion of psychoid. But Jung did not describe the psychoid as having specific properties – the gunas have specific qualities. Dasgupta proposed neutral monism or union of mind and matter as emerging from neutral gunas. Yoga or meditative practice helps in dissolution of mind-body dualism and helps in attaining pure consciousness (Dasgupta, 1941, pp. 179–194).

These details emphasize that any comparison between Indian notion of consciousness and Jung's notion of unconscious needs to place in context the distinction between philosophical, metaphysical and psychological categories. While it is outside the scope of this book to enumerate the differences between yoga philosophy and Jung's hermeneutic interpretation of kundalini yoga, it is useful to note that the religious and philosophical concept of Brahman and Jung's notion of Self would need to bring in the postulate of psychological unconscious or its lack, in Indian tenets, to make any effective comparison possible. In Jung's concept of the unconscious, consciousness is not surrendered nor is there a sublimation of opposites; a mediation between the two produces a transcendent third, or a new psychological attitude. In Indian tenets, a dissolution of the conflict is advocated for a perfected self. These differences account for the various irreconcilables and incommensurables in Jung's dialogues with Indian philosophers, and also the reason behind his distancing from the Indian standpoint. Jung was inspired by eastern religious principles and they offer a rich template for dialogue, but this is not fulfilled without attribution of differences. This is not to say that the notion of psyche is absent in ancient Indian knowledge; its expression is more in symbolic and mythological contents rather than theoretical, and its articulation is in speculative principles, rather than empirical phenomena. The metaphor of the animus, likewise, would be found more in symbols and myths rather than clinical and analytical studies. Analogies between Jung's contra-sexual concepts and symbols and metaphors of the animus necessitate, therefore, the inclusion of culture in understanding the psyche.

Location of Culture

Cultural theorist Homi K. Bhabha notes that with fluid and indeterminate states of culture outside binaries, it is no more fixed geography, race, gender or history that defines the location of culture (Bhabha, 1994). Beyond postmodernist, postfeminist, postcolonial definitions, it is the interstices or in-between realms, the borderlines of race, gender, geography, that constitute cultural spaces today. They are characterized by affiliative and contesting engagements, overlap and displacement of domains, and notions of selfhood and *nationness* that are not based on the past, or on inherited traditions. By logical extension, these interstitial spaces articulate differences and encourage hybridity. Bhabha identifies these emerging transnational spaces as interrogating histories, interrupting 'the performance of the present', and developing interstitial intimacy. Jung's history with India has features of interstitial dichotomy, ambivalences and paradoxes, as well as relatedness. Jung was more in sync with archetypal elements than with socio-political realities of history. The gap between ancient and modern is reduced in this volume, through interstitial spaces between contemporary events and past, and between social, heuristic knowing and preconceived thought.

The image of *ardhanarisvara* or Shiva and Parvati in union with their halved bodies aligned, has no psychological references in Indian knowledge. In ancient symbols of contra-sexuality, ardhanarisvara features predominantly. However, very little is discussed as to how a seamless union is achieved by this cosmic pair. Puranic myths describe various intersubjective dynamics of their relation, from which we draw impressions of a contra-sexual dyad. Bringing psychological nuances into religious myths alters their meaning, but enhances the myth's richness.

The nomadic and eccentric Shiva is often at odds with his wife, the charismatic Parvati, who has a will of her own. Her consort is notorious for being unkempt, dons an ash-smeared body, has bouts of rage, and prefers to move around on death grounds in the company of animals. In Hindu trinity, Shiva embodies chaos and destruction, and his unruly physical appearance mirrors his cosmic role. The beautiful Parvati had aspired for him when young, and sought him in marriage. Shiva's rugged exterior and turbulent nature hold very paradoxical abilities – he can rein in inchoate forces in the three worlds of earth, hell and heaven and is consulted by the gods during any emergent crisis. He sets in motion forces of destruction, so that new order may emerge. In a way, he prefigures creation. It is his ability to contain and transform tensions and paradoxes into creative gestalts that renders him central in Hindu theogony. It also endears him to Parvati. The animistic vitality that she displays as Durga while killing the demon Mahisasura in the myth of the goddess, is a trait close to Shiva's elemental nature. She is given a different name when she takes on this combative spirit.

Shiva and Parvati have an intricate dynamic that is both oppositional and unifying. A Puranic myth recounts that once when Shiva was away, Parvati created Ganesha from clayish residues, and anointed him as her son. Then she posted him at her doorstep and instructed him to prevent anyone from entering the house while she was conducting her daily ablutions. The dutiful boy stood at her doorstep, with the intent of guarding his mother. A wandering and disheveled Shiva returned home just then, after a long absence, and failed to recognize Ganesha. The boy had been playfully molded by Parvati, in her solitude, and had not been introduced to his father. On being barred entry into his own home by a stranger, Shiva was infuriated, and threatened to kill Ganesha. In the ensuing duel, he decapitated him, and proceeded to meet Parvati. The latter, suspecting that something untoward had happened, rushed out to find Ganesha's beheaded body. Parvati was grief-stricken and asked Shiva that Ganesha be restored to life. Shiva, who had by then come to know about the boy, tried to appease his wife, but failed. He had to take a head from one of his accompanying ganas and place it on Ganesha. The boy was revived, and went on to become the elephant-headed god of wisdom in Hindu pantheon.

The myth offers a template for viewing early childhood attachment relations, castration anxieties, Oedipal desires, but my focus is on the contra-sexual impulse that draws Shiva towards the benign and reclusive Parvati. It is symbolized in the image of the androgynous *ardhanarisvara*. The seemingly harmonious union veils an intricate dynamic. While

Parvati is engrossed in the inner quarters of her residence, preoccupied with caring for herself, Shiva is outside with his followers ambulating the world, overseeing dark and disordered realms. He is unaware of the changes that have occurred in his familial world in his absence. With this existential disconnect in place, he is unable to reach Parvati, is obstructed by Ganesha, and has to re-establish his relations with his family. But Shiva fails to see this at first, commits blunders and upsets his wife. A harmonizing of psychological states is necessary before any meaningful union can take place. In attempting to meet her in haste and by force, Shiva kills Ganesha. The boy is a gatekeeper to Parvati's world, and also her creation. In reviving Ganesha, Shiva foregoes his aggression and allows a new synergy to develop between himself and Parvati. He also establishes a bodily connect with his son and gives him a new head, symbolic of new wisdom.

In his Dream Analysis seminars of 1928, Jung deliberated about his patient whose virtuous outer life veiled a troubled inner life. The patient had brought his dreams to Jung, but it was revealed gradually that his obsession with social correctness, civility and decorum had turned his wife away from him, and made her frigid. She had no interest in him, as she was unable to live her life authentically under such high moral demands. This had pushed him to seek pleasures outside his marriage, in transgressive acts, which he then habitually tried to repress (Jung, 1984, p. 6). Shiva and Parvati's uniting dynamic encompasses separate personalities, but their longing for each other is constant. Their oppositions are held together in creative tension, and the couple navigate their differences together. The seamless union seen in the image of ardhanareshwara is not a preestablished, static harmony, but paths of negotiations in contra-sexual dyads that are shaped continuously. The image of ardhanareshwara seen below in a tenth-century sculpture, conveys the extraordinary vitality of this contra-sexual principle, centuries after its creation (Figure 5.1).

In *The Presence of Siva*, Stella Kramrisch writes that the essence of Shiva is both sacred and chaotized, destructive and holy, ascetic and erotic, wild and beautiful (Kramrisch, 1994). Sanskrit scholar and Indologist Sukumari Bhattacharji writes, 'Siva and Parvati cults drew close to each other until their merger is symbolically represented by the Ardhanarisvara image where the gods form two halves of one body. On the philosophical plane, this is a creative union of the active and passive principles. … It is one step in advance of the most primitive stage of mythical imagination when the mother-goddess was conceived as the procreatrix without male assistance. Moreover, most of these names are cognates derived from the same root, indicating that the pair is just one single undivided entity, self-cloven into two halves, like the protoplasm for the sake of creation. For Siva and Gauri this was a step to rise to the rank of the primordial pair and also to that of prime creators … . as Siva was assigned the

FIGURE 5.1 Ardhanarishvara – Shiva and Parvati.

Source: mark6mauno, CC BY 2.0, via Wikimedia Commons, https://commons.wikimedia.org/wiki/File:1_half_God_and_half_Goddess_Shiva_and_Parvati_Ardhanarishvara_Nepal_10th_century.jpg

specific task of destruction, his stature would be merely negative if he was not shown to be the creator as well. Here Parvati ... became his indispensable helpmate, and with her firmly implanted within his being the task became easier. Siva in his Ardhanarisvara personality was a very late mythological embodiment of the primordial bisexual creative principle' (Bhattacharji, 1970, p. 177).

In 'The Syzygy: Anima and Animus', Jung said that the syzygy consists of three elements – the feminine in man, the masculine in women and the masculine and feminine image that is integrated and symbolic, like a psychoid. The last cannot be consciously integrated into the personality (Jung, 1969a, para 41). The bisexual creative principle of ardhanareshwara or the image of Shiva and Parvati in union is a psychoid state that cannot be consciously adopted, but its psychological value can be discerned. Shiva tempers his aggression and dominance; Parvati too moves between outer and inner worlds, and the couple's fluid and changing dynamics are shaped through these contrasts.

There are radical differences in the way Vedic myths are viewed within the subcontinent. While classicists see them as resources for understanding human world, political anthropologist and subaltern historian Partha Chatterjee rejects their importance as critical sources of knowledge. He decries the notion of a singular Indian culture, especially one that is shaped by ancient, Aryan civilization. Chatterjee contends that classical past and Sanskrit literature do not acknowledge subaltern voice, and project Aryan history as the dominant cultural identity of India. He says that the notion of India's culture and history can neither be a construction of European Indological imagination, nor a romanticization of ancients, but needs to be articulated from within indigenous knowledge, from silenced and suppressed voices of marginalized social groups (Chatterjee, 1993). Alternate and secret histories, of the unrepresented underclass, are more significant, he argues. This is presented in several of the narratives in this volume – in Mahasweta's Dopdi, Phoolan, in Bharti's marginalized sexuality and Dalit status, in Rohan's feminized selfhood, and in the subjectivities of contemporary feminists.

I refer to this strand of historical theorizing and subaltern scholarship here since Jung's views about India were drawn from German romanticism and Oriental scholarship, and his inquiries of early Indological texts. These worlds were by no means ideal, free of colonizing and racist impulses, but synchronicities of history shaped Jung's links to the east in particular ways. His conception of the psyche as complex, paradoxical and synthesizing, aligns with the notion of culture that is heterogenous, plural and mutating. The creative and destructive character of the animus and its relation with culture is obscured in Jung's notions, but he consulted 'the other' in culture. The creative tension between archaic and contemporary, Vedic and subaltern, ancient and postcolonial, west and east, is erased when any one view is privileged. Jungian scholar Mark Saban notes that binary oppositions are not mutually exclusive categories. Jung placed his theoretical ideas between opposites of science and myth, rational and irrational, enchantment and disenchantment, without aligning himself with any one side, or hierarchizing either. It is reflected in his notion of Self, his alchemical writings and his theory of personality types. It was also present in his antinomial personality, central to the dynamic model of psyche that he evolved (Saban, 2012).

References

Atmanspacher, H. and Fuchs, C. A. (eds.) (2014) *The Pauli-Jung Conjecture and Its Impact Today*. Exeter: Imprint Academic.

Bhabha, H. K. (1994) *The Location of Culture*, 2nd ed. London: Routledge.

Bhattacharji, S. (1970) *The Indian Theogony: A Comparative Study of Indian Mythology from the Vedas to the Puranas*. Cambridge: Cambridge University Press.

Cambray, J. (2006) 'Towards the Feeling of Emergence', *Journal of Analytical Psychology*, 51, pp. 1–20.

Cambray, J. (2009) *Synchronicity: Nature and Psyche in an Interconnected Universe* (Carolyn and Ernest Fay Series in Analytical Psychology). College Station: Texas A & M University Press.

Chatterjee, P. (1993) *The Nation and its Fragments: Colonial and Post-Colonial Histories*. Princeton, NJ: Princeton University Press.

Clarke, J. W. (ed.) (1994) *Jung on the East*. London: Routledge.

Dasgupta, S. (1922) *A History of Indian Philosophy*. Cambridge: Cambridge University Press.

Dasgupta, S. (1941) 'Dogmas of Indian Philosophy' in *Philosophical Essays*. Calcutta: University of Calcutta.

Devi, M. (1994) *It Does not Die – A Romance*. Chicago: University of Chicago Press.

Dewaraja, L. (1996) 'Rhys Davids Memorial Lecture: "Haunted and pursued by the spiritual legacy bequeathed to him from Ceylon"', *Journal of the Royal Asiatic Society of Sri Lanka*, 41, New Series, pp. 1–12.

Eliade, M. (2009) *Yoga: Immortality and Freedom*. Bollingen Series LVI. Princeton, NJ: Princeton University Press.

Enz, C. P. (2010) *No Time to be Brief: A Scientific Biography of Wolfgang Pauli*. Oxford: Oxford University Press.

Geiser, S. (2005) *The Innermost Kernel: Depth Psychology and Quantum Physics. Wolfgang Pauli's Dialogue with C. G. Jung*. Berlin/Heidelberg: Springer Verlag.

Geiser, S. (ed.) (2019) *Dream Symbols of the Individuation Process: Notes of C. G. Jung's Seminars on Wolfgang Pauli's Dreams*. Philemon Foundation Series. Princeton, NJ: Princeton University Press.

Guggenbühl, C. (2008) 'Mircea Eliade and Surendranath Dasgupta: The History of Their Encounter', Unpublished paper, https://fid4sa-repository.ub.uni-heidelberg.de/149/1/Guggenbuehl_Eliade_DasGupta_Gesamt2.pdf.

Hogenson, G. B. (2005) 'The Self, the Symbolic and Synchronicity: Virtual Realities and the Emergence of the Psyche', *Journal of Analytical Psychology*, 50, pp. 271–284.

Jung, C. G. (1961) *Freud and Psychoanalysis*, Vol. 4, The Collected Works of C. G. Jung. Princeton, NJ: Princeton University Press.

Jung, C. G. (1969a) *Aion: Researches into the Phenomenology of the Self*, Vol. 9, pt. 2, The Collected Works of C. G. Jung. Princeton, NJ: Princeton University Press.

Jung, C. G. (1969b) *The Structure and Dynamics of the Psyche*, Vol. 8, The Collected Works of C. G. Jung. Princeton, NJ: Princeton University Press.

Jung, C. G. (1984) *Dream Analysis 1: Notes of the Seminar Given In 1928–30*. Edited by W. McGuire. Bollingen Series XCIX. Princeton, NJ: Princeton University Press.

Jung, C. G. (1989) *Memories, Dreams, Recollections*. Recorded and edited by Angela Jaffe. New York: Vintage Books.

Jung, C. G. (2018) History of Modern Psychology: Lectures Delivered at the ETH Zurich 1933–1934 in Shamdasani, S. (ed.). Princeton, NJ: Princeton University Press.

Kramrisch, S. (1994) *The Presence of Siva*. Mythos: The Princeton/Bollingen Series in World Mythology. Princeton, NJ: Princeton University Press.

Main, R. (2014) 'Synchronicity and the Problem of Meaning in Science' in', in Atmanspacher, H. and Fuchs, C. A. (eds.), *The Pauli-Jung Conjecture and Its Impact Today*. Exeter: Imprint Academic, pp. 217–240.

McGuire, W. and Hull, R. F. C. (1977). *C.G. Jung Speaking: Interviews and Encounters*. Bollingen Series XCVII. Princeton, NJ: Princeton University Press.

Meier, C. A. (ed.) (2001) *Atom and Archetype: The Pauli/Jung Letters 1932–1958*. London: Routledge.

Mueller, M. (1919) *The Six Systems of Indian Philosophy*. London: Longman, Green and Company.

Nandy, A. (1995) *Alternative Sciences: Creativity and Authenticity in Two Indian Scientists*. 2nd ed. New Delhi: Oxford University Press.

Nandy, A. (2009) *The Intimate Enemy: Love and Recovery of Self under Colonialism*. New Delhi: Oxford University Press.

Oldmeadow, H. (1995) 'C.G. Jung & Mircea Eliade: "Priests without Surplices"? Reflections on the Place of Myth, Religion and Science in Their Work'. *Talk delivered at the Bendigo Jung Society in 1992*. https://www.themathesontrust.org/papers/metaphysics/Jung%20&%20Mircea%20Eliade%20H%20Oldmeadow.pdf

Saban, M. (2012) 'The Dis/Enchantment of C.G. Jung', *International Journal of Jungian Studies*, 4(1), pp. 21–33.

Schopenhauer, A. (1913) *Transcendent Speculations on Apparent Design in the Fate of the Individual*. London: Watts.

Sengupta, S. (2013) *Jung in India*. New Orleans, LA: Spring Journal Books.

Shamdasani, S. (2003) *Jung and the Making of Modern Psychology: The Dream of a Science*. Cambridge: Cambridge University Press.

Skar, P. (2004) 'Chaos and Self-Organization: Emergent Patterns at Critical Life Transitions', *Journal of Analytical Psychology*, 49(2), pp. 243–262.

6

MATER COELESTIS

The Firmament of Becoming

In *Seven Sermons to the Dead* (Septem Sermones ad Mortuos), Jung wrote that spirituality is feminine; it conceives and embraces, unlike sexuality which is like the earthly father (Jung, 1989). While these dualities may not be considered as absolute, or viewed through fixed gender notions, it is worthwhile to note that Jung referred to the Gnostic term *pleroma* in explaining psychic opposites. The distinction between effective and ineffective, fullness and emptiness, difference and sameness, one and many, is what keeps human nature from dissolution or falling into perilous sameness. It is Principium Individuationis, the essence of human psyche that is not pleroma in itself, but opposites that manifest in the psyche (Jung, 1989, pp. 378–390). In the preceding chapters of this book, the phenomenon of the contra-sexual animus was traced in narratives of dissent and difference. The emergent animus has a spirit of discrimination. It is embodied in chthonic forces, in biophilic attributes, subversive behaviors and in impulses of self-actualization. The contra-sexual psyche does not manifest in dissent and divergence alone. It can be seen in transpersonal phenomena, in the realm of spirit, and in forces of culture. The story of an immigrant nun who arrived in India nearly a century ago, driven by a spirit of caritas, evokes the notion of feminine in *mater coelestis*. Its spontaneous appearance in the collective suggests a cultural synchronicity. Before we go into specifics of that story, a deliberation on the notion of individuation and the multiplicity of the animus as it manifests in the objective psyche.

A skyful of stars. A sun.
A world so spirited.

DOI: 10.4324/9780429423727-6

Somewhere in its midst
I have found, a place of my own,
And so, I sing in wonder.

The surge of an eternal time,
The ebb and flow of life
Throb in me, tug at my veins.

Feet on grassed path
I walk towards the woods,
The scent of flowers
Leaves me startled.
There is joy everywhere.

Ears on the ground, eyes open,
I pour myself
Looking for the unknown,
In all that is known.
In wonder, I sing.
— Rabindranath Tagore, 'Akashbhora' (2016),
author's translation from Bengali.

Tagore's song written in 1924, nearly a century ago, describes an evanescent moment, where the poet feels himself in sync with the world. It is not a concrete place that he signifies or the notion of a perfected life, but the image of a sentient being stirred by a lifeworld. The poet is mindful of the dualities of this image. The star-filled sky reminds him of his own solitariness, the stillness of heavens is a contrast to the vicissitudes of life, and the scent of unknown lingers around a familiar and accustomed earth. Tagore's feelings of awakening and wonder within these opposites, come close to Jung's description of 'world soul' or 'World Essence', that is the 'fiery spark of the soul of the world' or 'seeds of light broadcast in the chaos' (Jung, 1969, para 388). Jung linked such sparks with both lumen and numen, similar to the alchemical *scintillae*. Following fifteenth-century Swiss alchemist Paracelsus, Jung described the unconscious psyche as a star-strewn night sky or 'the starry vault of heaven' that holds the light of the inner body and the light of reason (Jung, 1969). It is *lumen naturae* that illumines the unconscious, like a luminous beam that erupts in the dark psyche.

Jung writes that individuation and collectivity are opposites that are related to each other by guilt (Jung, 1950, para 1099). He explains how conformity with the collective is the preferred path for individuals because separation necessitates the creation of something meaningful. Demands of individuation pull the individual away from collective into the personal world, but this retreat into oneself should yield certain objective values. The relation between an individual's inner life and the collective is therefore oppositional and compensatory. It contains dualities – social collaboration and outer development on one side, and the unconscious psyche and inner growth, on the other.

In 'The Self and Individuation', J.W.T Redfearn writes that Jung encountered these dualities in his life early on (Redfearn, 1977). From the enthroned phallus of his first dream, to the carved manikin that he kept in his attic, the image of an enormous turd that shattered the roof of a cathedral, to the stone in his garden that he mused upon, the inner other for Jung, was both terrifying and reassuring, intimate and alien. God was both divine and terrible, like the glittering roof of a cathedral of immense beauty to a strange, subterranean phallus (Jung, 1989, pp. 6–36). These opposites were present also in his mother's daytime and night-time personalities, in the solitude of his childhood years and their rich, intricate details that he reminisced later. They manifested in his two personalities, in his openness towards alien cultures as well as his contentious remarks on race and gender.

Oppositions and Unities

Jung found a unifying drive between opposites when he drew mandalas images (Jung, 1989, pp. 195–196), and in the mandalas his patients brought into analysis later. He viewed the yogasutras as denoting a unifying principle, but found that eastern connotations evoked in him feelings of *corpus alienum* (Jung, 1996, p. 14). Harold Coward has described the contrasts within the chakra images and their dynamic opposition (Coward, 1985, pp. 381–382). The root chakra is a dyad of a yellow square (earth) and an inverted triangle (Figure 6.1). A phallic stone rests in this square, encircled by an ascending serpent. A four-petalled red lotus borders the chakra, giving it structural unity. The lotus is a sign of consciousness, but in this early stage, consciousness is denoted as undifferentiated, with only few petals in bloom. In a subsequent chakra, six crimson lotus petals enclose a hemispherical white sphere (half-moon), while a golden lotus with twelve petals is seen in the fourth chakra enclosing two inverted triangles. In the fifth chakra, a sixteen-petalled lotus holds a circle and a white elephant. The contents of the chakras change with every ascension, with the petals multiplying in number. The sixth chakra is symbolized by dual forces of phallus and *yoni*, circled by two white petals. In the final chakra, even this duality is transcended and a thousand-petalled illumined golden lotus, blooms over a circle (Figure 6.1). Jung's approach to the kundalini chakras was not its philosophical underpinnings but its ontological essence, or what he conceived as the psyche's progression towards consciousness through a reconciling of dualities. Tagore experienced the self as synchronized with the world, in rare and liminal moments of awakening. Jung saw it as opposites that do not dissolve into sameness, but progress towards complex orders of consciousness.

FIGURE 6.1 Muladhara Chakra.

Source: Author's collection, artist unknown.

With this view of the individuating Self in the background, a complex expanse is implicated in the trajectory of the animus. Its emergence is tied to unconscious contra-sexuality, repression of the feminine in culture and dissent and opposition in inner and outer worlds. A radical force surfaces in the psyche compensation, to balance what is absent or repressed in the unconscious. A loosening of the conscious attitude and an *abaissement du niveau* mental allows unconscious contents to emerge, that seek to offset psyche's one-sidedness. The emergent contents are assimilated gradually and can produce expanded consciousness or new psychological attitudes, in time. Opposites are brought into relation, and a reorganization of the individual's inner and outer worlds occurs. The dynamic reorganization of opposites within the chakra symbols symbolizes an individuation principle, that Jung believed was in the repository of the ancients, and in archaic knowledge.

Cultural Correspondences

In 'The Snake in the Mandala' (Jones, 2020), Raya Jones examines Jung's interpretation of a series of mandala images that were brought to him during the course of a patient's analysis. Jung described them as part of the patient's individuation process, in which twenty-four paintings show variously paired objects during different stages of analysis. The images of snake, sphere, stone, wind, a flash of lightning, objects like pyramids, squares and zodiacal figures were believed to have emerged spontaneously in the patient's psyche when she was experiencing a life predicament. At one point in the series, a sphere is seen pierced by a phallic snake. Jung surmised this to be a loosening of the patient's psyche, which had been governed until then by excess rationality. The mandalas transform after the snake pierces the sphere, and after a flash of lightning explodes a stone. Raya Jones questions Jung's use of the notion of collective unconscious in his interpretation of these images. I note merely that they reveal surprising parallels with kundalini chakra symbols and other Gnostic imagery. Jung's amplification of dream symbols using alchemical references seemed inspired by wider cultural factors.

In the *muladhara* or root chakra, for example, the tip of the triangle is seen aimed at an elephant, and resembles an arrowhead (Jung, Shamdasani, 1996, Introduction, see Image 2. Muladhara Chakra). In Indian religious mythology, the seven-tusked mythical elephant *Airavata* is considered a symbol of consciousness. The arrow that touches the elephant in the root chakra is parallel to the serpent that perforates the sphere in Jung's patient's mandala. The root chakra has a snake coiled around a phallic stone; the stone and snake are encircled by a lotus, i.e., opposites inhering within a whole. The uniting symbol of the lotus is constant in all the constellations of the chakras.

In Jung's patient's mandala, the stone is struck by a flash of lightning. This is evocative of the work of sixteenth-century medieval mystic Jacob Boehme (1575–1628), about whom Jungian scholar John Dourley writes in 'The Religious Implications of Jung's Psychology' (Dourley, 1995). Jung's patient's drawings were separated from Boehme's imagery by three centuries, but there is a correspondence between them. 'In Boehme's imagery this flash is ignited when the dark divine fire unites with its redeeming light, or when the redeeming light penetrates its dark opposite' (Dourley, 1995, p. 197). The inert stone and the flash of lightning are opposites uniting; Eliade described such unity as homologizing of opposites. Jung called it the pleroma from where opposites are evoked. Tagore referred to it as dualism and non-dualism, finite and infinite, or opposites that do not exclude each other. They coexist in ways where neither is reduced or erased. 'To darkness are they doomed who worship only the body, and to greater darkness they who worship only the spirit' (Isha Upanishad).

Jung's painting 109 in The Red Book (The Man of Matter) of an earthly man impaled by a golden ray of light suggests a similar incision. The serpent is killed in the process. It signified the umbilical cord of a new birth, Jung wrote (Jung, 2009, p. 109). In the chakras, the serpent is not annihilated, but is transformed through interactions with the other. Eastern alchemical symbols, in particular the serpent, have mythical and religious connotations that are distinct from Christian symbols. In Vedic mythology, Shiva dons a coiled serpent in his matted hair, while Vishnu reclines on a cosmic snake in the milky ocean. Jung's observation that mandalas hold opposites and tension of opposites is reflected in the symbology of the chakras, and also in the contrasting symbology in eastern and western religions. In eastern symbols, the snake has intrinsic value, and its energy is transformed from dark to light, while in Jung's image in The Red Book, the serpent is at first annihilated. Jung used the images and symbols in The Red Book for dialogue with the psyche, but in eastern symbols, the notion of psychological unconscious is not implicated in chakra meditations.

Jung was in active dialogue with the images in The Red Book. He had completed working on them by the time *A Study in the Process of Individuation* was published in 1934; it was based on his analysis of his patient, Kristine Mann. In 1932, Jung had lectured on Kundalini Yoga at the Psychology Club along with Indologist Wilhelm Hauer. Mann's close colleague, Dr. Eleanor Bertine attended these seminars. Further still, Toni Woolf's lecture on 'Tantric symbolism in Goethe' in March 1932, preceded Jung's lectures that same year. Jung also lectured on '*Westliche Parallelen zu den Tantrischen Symbolen*' (Western Parallels to Tantric Symbols) in October 1932 (Jung, 1996, p. xi). These concurrences show that by early 1930s Jung was aware of mandala symbolism of the east, and the parallels detected may have reinforced his use of the notion of collective unconscious in dream interpretations. The point I draw here is that these symbols have cultural parallels, and Jung was deeply aware of this fact. He emphasized archetypal similarities and cultural parallels more than personal contents of the unconscious.

The Self-Organizing Psyche

Jungian analyst Patricia Skar in 'Chaos and Self-organization: Emergent Patterns at Critical Life Transitions' notes that individuation processes in dynamic systems reveal psyche's self-organizing tendency, or the ability to produce complex systems of meaning from prevailing chaos (Skar, 2004). The capacity to self-organize implies psyche's ability to change its internal structure, in order to adapt to a new environment. Such spontaneous re-structuring of contents with increasing complexity is seen in the chakra symbols of kundalini yoga. Colors change from intense red, purple and blue to sheer white, and multiple forms emerge as triangles align with circles and squares. The kundalini snake symbolized near the coccyx in the root chakra is not visible in the higher chakras, but the lotus is consistent in its presence, multiplying as it ascends. The contrasts between the objects, of earth and moon, snake and stone, square and circle, yoni and lingam, converge in a radiant beam of light in the highest chakra.

Although yoga psychology lays emphasis on introversion and concentration *(tapas)*. Skar thinks that dynamic psyche's self-organization requires intimate links with the environment and a relational outer world for restructuring of its contents. She highlights that the archetype's self-organizing potential is seen in critical life transitions, when unconscious complexes are constellated spontaneously in the psyche. But psyche's self-organization occurs in relation to its environment, making the archetype an emergent relational entity rather than pre-existent and *a priori*. This has been emphasized by others as well. In Indian religious philosophy, the chakras are denoted *a priori* symbols of consciousness, with introvertive practices that stimulate its emergence. Mircea Eliade writes in 'Yoga: Immortality and Freedom', 'From the Upanishads onward, India has been seriously preoccupied with but one great problem, – the structure of the human condition. ... the multiple "conditionings" of the human being; ... the problem of the temporality and historicity of man; ... and the anxiety and despair that inevitably follow upon consciousness of temporality' (Eliade, 1958, p. xxx). In Eliade's view, the notion of consciousness in Vedic symbolism is Brahman or axis mundi, the cosmic pillar or *skambha* that stands at the center of this world and connects the underworld to the earth and heavens. It is the totality of the psyche, an ontological foundation for wholeness (Eliade, 1958, p. 115). By virtue of its links to the underworld, the self also includes the unconscious, but its psychological dynamics are not discussed in Indian tenets. In its emphasis on solitude and reflection, the yoga system differs from Skar's idea of a relational outer world, necessary for psyche's self-organization.

While it is true that therapeutic processes encourage self-reflexivity and concentration on inner-world phenomena, analytic encounters are structured around transference and counter-transference dynamics, in interactions between analyst and analysand, and these are not solo exercises. Jung's references to alchemical symbols in yoga philosophy are therefore in its symbolic essence, not to be conflated with practical methods of therapy. Although, introvertive yoga meditation can be effective accompaniment to therapeutic processes, one does not substitute the other. Skar's argument that critical life events engender psychic transitions by pushing the individual ego to adapt to new realities, ties inner psychic dynamics with outer world and is distinct from yoga's solitary, inward-looking methods. The narratives in the preceding chapters, locate contra-sexual motifs of the animus in relational social worlds, in collective and cultural forces, with the latter often acting as catalysts for feminine emergence and transcendence. Inner opposites are manifested in outer oppositional figures, and the tension of opposites often produces cathartic transformations in the psyche. The feminine is embodied in the psyche, in culture, in experiences of the other, in men and masculine, and in numerous strands of outer and inner. It is not only in the dynamics of inner contents that individuating trajectories are shaped, but in the interaction of the individual psyche with its environment. The outer world, and the individual's links to the collective are proposed in Indian philosophy through specific ontologies, outside yoga philosophy.

Jung's Stages of Life

Skar has argued that the notion of individuation implicates a relational outer world. Jung emphasized a dialectical relation between individual and collective. Although Jung focussed more on intrapsychic elements, he acknowledged the place of collective psyche, and defined it as psychic contents of mankind in general, not just worldly ideas but subjectivity, feelings and moral consciousness (Jung, 1971, para 692). Roger Brooke describes the psyche as intersubjective and phenomenological. The psyche is not an encapsulated, solipsistic entity but a lifeworld that is existentially spatial like Husserl's *Lebenswelt* (Brooke, 2015, p. 82). While this is true, for Jung, the relation between individual and collective is antithetical, even when connected. This dialectic holds possibilities of widening of individual consciousness. The existence of problems brings about growth of consciousness (Jung, 1969, para 750). The widening of consciousness was not the goal of the collective, and hence a tension existed between the two. The problems of the psyche rise from within the individual, Jung thought, and so individuation implies knowledge of these inner contents rather than collective ideas.

Jung's singular emphasis on intrapsychic dynamics may be reconsidered today, since the phenomenon of the psyche (and the animus) implicates an outer world, and occurs in the dynamics of both, the individual and collective. Contra-sexual tensions are embodied in the collective, as well as personal, in forces outside the individual and within. The Self organizes itself in interaction with this environment reconciling various inner and outer polarities, attempting to find coherence within these tensions. Opposites are integral to differentiation. Jung outlined different life stages for harmonizing psychological opposites. He characterized these individuating stages with differing consciousness (Jung, 1969). The first stage of consciousness is always anarchic, with islands of scattered perception, and no continuous memory. This is followed by a monistic stage of ego consciousness. The first stage being in childhood, the second stage of ego development is in a person's prime. The recognition of crucial problems occurs in the third stage, in midlife. Jung gave less importance to childhood and old age compared to ego development in the second stage, and the notion of Self in the third. In conceiving the Self, individuation and the life stages, Jung used cultural parallels and archetypal constructs. Michael Fordham reminisced about Jung's proclivity towards the archetypal in a JAP article of 1975: 'At a dinner party I tried to start a discussion of child therapy, and Jung conceded that children's dreams could be of scientific interest because they showed so much evidence in favor of this theory of the collective unconscious' (Fordham, 1975, p. 108).

The central problem in the journey of consciousness according to Jung, is the surfacing of problems in midlife. The individual resists this development, and clings to an inferior consciousness, or false and exaggerated notions about the world, believing them to be unchangeable truths. Distressing thoughts and experiences are repressed, and this triggers in the individual a neurotic disconnect with the inner world. Jung compared this to the sun's diurnal orbit, where brightness reigns in the first half and darkness emerges later. The descent into the dark brings a reversal of libido, and a desire to withdraw into oneself.

It is imaginable that such an ambivalent account of the psyche that tends to reverse its own course from light to dark, from concrete worldly goals to unknown fantasies, would generate anxiety and resistance in the individual, pursuing the security of a familiar world. But Jung emphasized that the ascendence of the unconscious in the second half of life was inevitable, and also inordinately significant. He thought that this was known to the ancients, and therefore a supramundane goal of life was conceived in the notion of afterlife (Jung, 1969, para 790). By this he did not imply an ontological notion of immortality or afterlife, but a psychic telos that encourages a person to approach the second half of life purposefully. The goal of the second half of life is not ego strengthening, but knowledge of a transpersonal entity called Self.

With regard to the phenomenology of the animus, life stages suggest reconciliation of familiar, conscious contents of the psyche with alien, unconscious contra-sexual other. The other manifests discretely in each individual, and shapes the individuating trajectory, unique to each individual telos. Its archetypal expression is in stories of Durga, Phoolan, Dopdi, Bharti, Rohan, where sexual, gender, social or ideological other is encountered. Each of the protagonists encountered these inner and outer forces. Interaction with them induced radical developments in the individual, suggesting the fluid and mutating quality of the animus. The developmental aspects of the archetype, that is constantly in interaction with the environment, shaping and transforming the psyche, is not articulated distinctly in Jung's theorizing.

Four Stages of Life in Indian Religious Thought

Ancient Vedic religion has in fact structured human life in four stages in the concept of *ashrama*. Classical scholar and philologist Patrick Olivelle says that *ashrama* is a theological construct whose meaning should be located within Brahmanical hermeneutics (*Mīmāṃsā* philosophy). Etymologically, *ashrama* means to be in toil and labor since it contains the word *shrama* (labor), but mythically, it evokes the image of the creator (Prajapati) laboring to create the world. The term *ashrama* signifies a specific mode of life that involves ritual exertions and sacrifices; it can also be a specific place where certain meditative practices are followed. While both location and practice characterize the concept of *ashrama*, its symbolic essence could be the human being's quest for meaning and consciousness (Olivelle, 1993).

Olivelle maintains that ashrama in Brahmanical religion does not indicate different stages of life, but a specific mode of life chosen by the individual (Olivelle, 1993, p. 31). He notes that psychoanalysts and historians like Sudhir Kakar and Romila Thapar have erroneously interpreted it as a concept of human development through life stages, or ordering of human life-cycle by an integration of opposites. Without detracting from Olivelle's theological interpretations, I would like to say that the four stages of the Vedic *ashrama* can be compared with Jung's concept of life stages, and also differentiated from it. Hermeneutically, the four life stages of ashrama can be seen as integrating various dualities of conscious and unconscious, inner and outer.

Ancient ashrama begins with an initiation phase where the student pursues learning under a teacher. In this, the student is required to live with other initiates, in proximity of the teacher. On reaching adulthood and completing studies, the student takes on the role of a householder. He is responsible for making a place in the world and nurturing a family, putting into practice the education he has acquired. The third phase is retreat into the forests, after the individual has completed his familial duties and fulfilled his worldly goals. Pursuit of social goals is not important in the third stage, and the individual's attention turns to those issues which he has ignored till then. In this stage, the person seeks a higher purpose and meaning of life, beyond collective values. In the fourth and final phase, the individual adopts a life of a renunciate, where he involves himself with questions about death and his transition into the next world. The ashrama in Indian theology is conceived keeping a male initiate's life in view, not an ordinary Brahmin but an extraordinary person, who is able to follow the rigorous practices of this philosophy.

Olivelle points out that the theological interpretation of ashrama is that the individual chooses one of these modes as a primary way of experiencing life, rather than experiencing all four stages in succession. Psychologically, this may be understood as a particular attitude and typological orientation determining the individual's course of life. Emphasis on learning and acquiring knowledge may be preferred over active intervention and work in the outer world, if the intuitive, introverted function is dominant in the individual. Family, domestic ties and worldly desires may be central to those who adopt the householder path; others may choose service to a cause as a primary life mode. A *puer aeternus* type may be imbued with a state of youthfulness and may not transition through the life stages in normative ways. A positive puer attitude predisposes the individual towards generativity, while a negative puer keeps the individual attached to infantile desires.

Early childhood attachment relations, especially resolution of parental complexes, are crucial for the individual's successful transition through life stages, engagement with the world and adoption of healthy social goals. Successful transition through life stages suggests psychological maturation and growth. In current contexts of gender non-conformity, heteronormative goals of marriage and children need not be considered essential. The second stage can imply strengthening of ego through establishing one's identity in the collective, and in creative work. The third stage brings a life of contemplation, withdrawal from collective values, and inquiry about the inner world. This stage of *ashrama* coincides with Jung's notion of the second half of life. The transition from an extraverted outer life to an introverted reflective state may be disconcerting, and could be triggered through unexpected life events or crises. The transition is necessary as it remedies the individual's one-sided focus in the outer world. In both theological and psychological approaches, the stages are conceived as fluid, transitional and diverse, constellating in distinct ways. Patrick Olivelle states, 'The householder's asrama, consequently, is not necessarily a permanent state, and the hermit's asrama is not necessarily a celibate state' (Olivelle, 1993, p. 113). Although Olivelle's interpretation is theological and distinct from psychological or social approaches, its hermeneutic essence can be compared to Jung's notion of individuation. An individual transitions from one stage to another by overcoming various tensions and polarities. Consequently, the constellation of contra-sexual complexes in the unconscious psyche may direct an individual's psychological maturation in a certain way, with his individuation geared towards resolving these complexes in ways that are meaningful to individual telos.

Ashrama and Jung's Stages of Life – A Comparative View

Jung's own life (1875–1961) may be viewed from within this hermeneutic model. While his 'First Years' (1875–1900) of childhood, school and university may signify an initiation phase, his marriage, early career at Burgholzli hospital, and his relations with Freud (1900–1913) formed the second important phase of his life. This phase gave him a foothold in his profession, established his family life, and oriented him to alternate knowledge traditions. Jung's transition into the third stage (1913–1944) began with his separation from Freud, and with his 'Confrontation with the Unconscious'. It triggered in him a search for his own myth, a distancing from mainstream psychoanalytic theories, work on The Red Book, fostering of analytical psychology as a discipline, and developing of his signature concepts.

The third quarter also witnessed the building of Bollingen Tower in 1922. The Tower was for him a place of maturation, where he could become what he was destined to be (Jung, 1989, p. 225). Jung's transition into the third phase occurred through a period of inner turmoil. He had resigned from the editorship of Jahrbuch, and the International Psychoanalytic Association in 1914. He had also resigned from Zurich University. This period was marked by his separation from mainstream psychoanalytic schools, travel outside Europe, and publications of his major concepts. Jungian analyst Lance Owens writes, 'During the same period, he was increasingly disillusioned with theoretical constructs about the origin and nature of unconscious contents—a disenchantment that led to termination of his six-year misadventure with Freud.' Jung wrote in the draft manuscript of Liber Novus that what he had previously considered his soul was not at all the soul, but a dead system that he had contrived (Owens and Hoeller, 2014, p. 3).

Jung's transition into the fourth phase manifested in his illness of 1944. He was sixty-nine years old when his health deteriorated suddenly and left him bedridden. In the ensuant visions that he had while being laid up in bed, on more than one occasion he encountered the image of a *yogi* (Jung, 1989, pp. 289–299). In one vision, he saw himself in an empyrean realm, with a view of the globe, gloriously illuminated in blue. From far above, the silvery outlines of the subcontinent of India and Ceylon were visible, as well as the snow-capped Himalayas. While Jung stood contemplating on this scene, various other continents came into view. When he turned southwards, a large black stone became visible, floating near him; its entrance had been hollowed to form a chamber. A black Hindu yogi in lotus posture awaited his arrival at the entrance. Inside, thousand oil lamps lit the pathway. As he crossed the threshold, an extraordinary sensation gripped Jung. It seemed as if his entire earthly life was being stripped away from him through painful extraction, leaving behind its essence. Crossing the threshold of the temple implied a transition, as in Indian temples and traditional households, one typically enters a new space through an intermediate doorway, which are specially designed and symbolizes transition into a new space. Jung was engulfed by opposing feelings of emptiness and fullness during this crossing. He felt bereft of desire but had an objective understanding of his life. The vision indicated that a transition was imminent. Although Jung experienced intense resistance in recovering from his illness and resuming his everyday life, when he eventually recouped, he experienced a very fruitful and creative period of work. He felt reconciled with the contents of his life and had an objective view of his destiny (Jung, 1989, p. 291).

Jung's transition into the last quarter of life was prefigured in this dream, where the presence of a yogi at a temple threshold signified a crossing. In eastern religion, guru is a mediator between the human and transcendent world, one who facilitates transitions. Its symbolization in an alien cultural image signified for Jung, a yet unachieved life goal. It symbolized wholeness, but also a psychic state that is completely alien and opposed to the western mind (Jung, 1989, p. 324). The final phase for Jung involved consolidation of his lifework and contemplation about the objective essence of his life. The publication of some of his most important works during this period, as well as *Memories, Dreams, Reflections*, coincided with this transition. Jung contended that most of the contents of the fourth stage were close to the eastern concept of Maya or illusion. But Jung's questions about self and wholeness, the peculiar contents of his destiny, marked the fourth phase of his life – a quaternity, through a squaring of the Mandala. This summary shows that Jung's conception of the stages of life is distinct from the ancient theory of ashrama, although they present compelling analogies.

In the chapter *'The Stages of Life'*, Jung identified the four stages of psychic life – childhood, youth, midlife and extreme old age as important crossroads of consciousness. The passage from one stage to another, entails struggle with opposites, resistance to entering new, unfamiliar worlds, and these were experienced by Jung during his illness. He denoted childhood and old age as devoid of conscious contents. (Jung, 1969, para 795). This is arguable, since attachment relations, parental complexes, childhood traumas, influence the individual's ability to successfully transition into adulthood.

Jung's emphasis that the second half of life is significant for ego development is in contrast to the third phase, where the focus is not on the ego, but on the Self. Stepping into the householder stage necessitates an adaptation to collective values. Stepping away from it brings a shift of attention from the outer to the inner. The third phase encourages reflection about what constitutes one's particular life path. It entails a relinquishing of all that has been held close in the second quarter, a reappraisal of one's life and a quest for new values. The third quarter brings an aversion towards the mundane. It seeks to inquire into the objective essence of one's lifeworld. The stages of life are not envisioned as similar for every individual. The comparisons between Jung's stages of life and the Indian ashrama system are described below (Table 6.1).

In a 2008 posthumously published paper titled 'Your Self: Did You Find It or Did You Make It?', Jungian analyst Louis Zinkin (1926–1993), wrote about apparent contradictions in Jung's notion of the objective psyche or collective unconscious. Jung's notion of Self-formed through opposites does not clarify if the Self is pre-existent or socially constructed, solitary or

TABLE 6.1 Comparative View of *Ashrama* and Jung's Stages of Life

Four Life Modes of Ashrama – *Theological*	*Jung's Stages of Life – Psychological*
Artha, Kama, Dharma and *Moksha* constitute *Purushartha* or the four goals of life. They can be translated as Wealth, Pleasure, Ethics and Spiritual Liberation.	Jung identified life stages for individuation. The first half of life is devoted to development of the ego. The second half is aimed for the development of Self.
Four distinct life modes are suggested in ashrama. These are not life stages, that occur sequentially and uniformly for all.	In Jungian psychology, the four life stages are deemed as sequential. Jung prioritized two of them.
Any of the four modes of the ashrama may be adopted by the individual as a life goal. Life modes are distinct from life stages.	Jung gave less importance to the first and last stages of life. Emphasis is on first half of life and second.
First life mode is initiation or learning under a teacher.	The first stage is in childhood. Jung did not give much emphasis to the contents of this stage.
Second is householder – the path of marriage, pursuit of worldly goals, establishing oneself in the collective.	The second stage of life is crucial for ego development - establishing one's identity in the world and adaptation to the collective.
Third life mode is called retreat into the forests – distancing from worldly life and path of contemplation	The second half of life that involves separating oneself from collective goals and reflection on Self.
Fourth life mode is renunciation or asceticism – pursuit of spiritual goals, solitude.	Search for wholeness, consolidation of lifework. Intimations of the transcendent.

multiple, if it is essentially unknowable and impersonal, or needs universal validation (Zinkin, 2008). Further, Zinkin notes that Jung's notion of Self derives its meaning from an archetypal basis which is a contrast to personal psyche, internal objects and intersubjectivity. The archetypal basis of Jung's theorizing can be discerned from cultural parallels that Jung found. In describing the life stages, Jung elaborated on their psychological meaning, and not their theological value.

Zinkin's constructivist views of the Self in relation to the world is significant. The four modes of the ashrama signify the individual's relation to the collective, even though the quest for truth encourages the individual's distancing from worldly goals and cultivation of an inward attitude. Ashrama modes are not described through personal psychology, although one can envisage that specific modes will be adopted by individuals and implicates the personal. In Jung's life stages, as well as in the Indian principle dualities and tensions of erotic and spiritual, earthly and transcendent, inner and outer are suggested. This locates human experience not only in ordinary everyday world, but also in a transpersonal realm. Spirit and matter are not separated, and the ability to hold these dualities is crucial. Individuation is strapped in a relation between a present moment and an evanescent time, self and the world, body and soul, personal and collective, where intricacies of the particular are not lost in the whole. The following narratives trace the phenomenon of the animus in individual psyche, in personal and subjective realms, and in the archetypal. Feminine individuation are often channeled through violent initiations, and through encounter of destructive, contrasexual figures.

Bluebeard Man – Vital Initiations

Charles Perrault's 'Bluebeard' is a French folktale written in 1697, that tells the story of a wealthy nobleman who is on the lookout for a bride. The man had a blue beard, and this peculiar mark made women wary of him. There was also a rumor that he had married several other women before, but no one knew about their whereabouts. One day, having fancied his neighbor's pretty daughters, the bluebeard man asked their mother if he could marry one of the daughters. He invited the ladies to his estate, and after a weeklong of merrymaking, the women felt at ease with him. The man was not so strange after all, they thought. As it happened, the younger daughter agreed to the marriage. A month after the wedding, the bluebeard man declared that he had to go on tour and handed over the keys of his castle to his bride. He asked her to please herself with all his riches, meet friends, make merry, enter every part of the castle, except the last room on the ground floor. The key to that room was small, but the man forbade his wife from opening it, and warned her of dire consequences if she did.

But the young wife was less inclined towards enjoying the pleasures her husband had suggested for her, and more curious about the room that she had been forbidden to enter. Soon, she had climbed down the stairs of the house to enter that chamber. When she opened its door, she found to her horror, dead bodies stacked across the floor with blood everywhere. The key fell out of her hand as she trembled, at the grisly scene before her. She managed to retrieve the key and return to her room, but to her dismay, the key was smeared with blood and the stains would not go. The bluebeard man returned sooner than expected, and found out from the bloodstained key that his wife had disobeyed him. She had to die he said, but the bride pleaded to be given some time. Alone in the tower, she prayed that her brothers arrive and rescue her. Two horsemen riding at a distance turned out to be her brothers, and she was rescued at the nick of time. The bluebeard man was killed, the bride rescued, and we are told that the tale ends happily.

This is a story about the contra-sexual masculine other. The flamboyant bluebeard man has a deep, dark secret that he stubbornly guards. He is on the lookout for a bride whose innocence will lead her to him and to the uncovering of this ominous secret. The secret, when discovered, allows him to fulfil his desire of murdering innocent young brides. As usually happens in such cases, the young woman is not as interested in her husband's wealth, as she is in the forbidden chamber of his castle. The animus, seeks dark and dangerous secrets in the hidden psyche. The feminine does not merely inspire and emotionalize a man, but leads him to the dark recesses of the unconscious, and all that a person hides under a colorful persona. The contents of the underground chamber horrify the bride, but her secret is intended to be revealed. Hence, the blood-smeared key cannot be wiped clean, and her transgression discovered.

Walter Odajnyk notes in 'Archetypal Interpretation of Fairy Tales: Bluebeard' (Odajnyk, 2004), that the bluebeard man symbolizes a chthonic masculine, a nonhuman entity, whose contact with nubile young women provokes necessary psychic transformation in the masculine. He is part of a quaternity, that has three feminine figures, the mother and two daughters. We notice that there is no personal ground for the bluebeard man's antagonism towards his bride; its contents are of an impersonal nature. He has a distant aura, and the strange rumors about him emphasize his impersonality. The repressed contents of his personality are stored deep underground, as dead bodies in a forbidden chamber of his castle, whose key is also small.

The discovery of these bodies leads to tragic consequences for the bride. Her life had till then been confined to the familiar world of her mother and sister, in one-sided experiences of the feminine. The bluebeard man's dark and devious nature is an unknown other, although other women had been wary of him and his strange blue beard. His sinister character is a contrast to her naivety. Entering the blood-soaked chamber, she discovers an archetypal scene of murder, a dark and macabre secret, that puts her life in danger. When faced with the threat of death, the bride can rescue herself only with the help of her brothers, as her self-agency is yet undeveloped. The brothers offer a contrasting masculine pole, symbolizing the life-giving character of the archetype, against its destructiveness.

It can be imagined that had the story continued, the young woman's discovery of her husband's identity would involve a painstaking confrontation with the contents of the hidden chamber. It would be a secret whose significance would be difficult to comprehend or convey. Jung struggled with his secrets, his initiatory dreams and childhood games, which he could not bear to reveal to others. Not till he was in his sixties did he begin to talk about them. The secret brings the treasured feeling of individuality, that she or he feels compelled to guard (Jung, 1989, p. 342). The secret acts like a shield against the individual's submergence in the collective, providing a place for deliberating on the peculiar contents of one's personality. The young woman's discovery of a secret would threaten her inner world, and would be difficult to reconcile with. Although she had been asked by her husband to stay within certain limits, she had chosen to venture into the unknown. Having made a horrific discovery there, it would not be possible for her to go back to the innocence of her earlier life. The experience of the other would transform her, as it had done for Phoolan, Dopdi, Bharti and Rohan. They had encountered the other, before they came into their own. It was not only the strange and alien other that they encountered, but awareness about evil, and its place in the world. The mystery of the bloodstained chamber would be assimilated when the young bride would find a relationship with its contents, that would transform her nascent consciousness to a more differentiated state of being.

In an ancient Indian Puranic myth, the child god Krishna is reprimanded by his mother Yashoda for having consumed dirt while playing. When Krishna denies having done so and asks her to examine his mouth, a flustered Yashoda peers inside to find a strange scene – the entire universe held inside his tiny mouth, the planetary orb, all of nature, and even dirt, lying in its midst. It is a harmonized co-existence of matter, the image of anima mundi or Brahman. As an avatar of Vishnu, Krishna wished to show his earthly mother a glimpse of the universe in all its compositeness, of which dirt and soil were a part, existing in relation to the whole.

The hidden and secluded room of the bluebeard man, on the other hand is separated from his outer life, its repressed contents existing in an unrelated whole. The need to have this room discovered and brought in contact with the world impels his pursuit of innocent, young women. It holds mutilated and dismembered parts of his psyche, a primal scene of murder and violence. Its gruesomeness leaves the bride shaken, and its enormity suggests not just individual acts of slaughter or episodic murders, but archetypal violence. Such acts of violence were found in rape and killing of the feminine, in the chapter on Phoolan. Meeting this contra-sexual stranger brings the bride in contact with the instinctual psyche, confrontation with it, instead of isolation and repression of the other.

Christian Evangelism in a Hindu Heartland

The phenomenon of the animus in the personal psyche is distinct from its manifestation in culture. John Dourley in 'The Religious Implications of Jung's Psychology' (Dourley, 1995) notes that the psychogenetic origins of religious experience make intrapsychic dialogues possible. Religious revelations and visionary experiences are compensatory phenomena, as psyche's key dynamic is the affirmation of the unity of consciousness. Hence, if the personal or collective psyche is imbued with rationality and materiality, its compensatory dynamic or 'archetypal redress' would be the eruption of supernatural, spiritual or transcendental. Dourley states that Jung's dialogues with Jewish theologian Martin Buber and English Dominican priest Victor White disintegrated when Jung's view of religious experience having a psychological basis, was emphasized. Jung's ideas were incompatible with western monotheistic thought, with charges of reductionism and psychologism leveled against him frequently.

Jung's response was fairly uniform in these situations. He affirmed that he was an empiricist, and religious symbols were of psychological value to him, especially when his patients experienced them in their dreams and fantasies. Without an experiential basis, religious ideas were dogma, at best metaphysical postulates. Dourley notes that Jung's notion of evil similarly, was not the absence of good or *privatio boni*, but evil that had a psychological basis. Dialogues with Victor White affirmed that the demonic, instinctual, bodily and feminine elements were split off from Christian God image. The notion of psychological Self served as a uniting symbol in such a scenario, *tertium non datur,* or the third function between opposites. This was not acceptable to Victor White. Nor for Buber, for whom the absolute other was beyond psyche. For Jung, it was in the depths of unconscious life. In a way, these differences were not very unlike the conflicts Jung faced with Indian philosophers in the decade of the thirties.

Dourley's notion of Christ as a helpful masculine figure that engenders spiritual flowering in women, seen in the lives of medieval mystics like Mechthild von Macdeburg, does not take into account possible differences between psychological and religious. Instances of female mystics in spiritual union with male gods are not uncommon in India, especially sixteenth century Indian hagiographic legends of Bhakti saints, like Mirabai. But the subjective and personal contents of these lives are largely unknown. Without knowledge of intrapsychic and interpsychic dynamics, the psychological contents of these phenomena cannot be located.

This is evident in the story of Mother Teresa (1910–1997) whose astonishing life in India and work among the poor and destitute of Calcutta, convey curious synchronicities of culture and history. Her biographical narrative offers very little glimpse of the personal life of the celebrated missionary. Meg Greene's *Mother Teresa* tells us about the author's frustrating experience of historicizing a life where little is known about the inner subjective experiences of her childhood, family and personal world (Greene, 2004). Agnes Gonxha Bojaxhiu was born in the little-known town of Skopje in Albania in 1910, in a middle-class household, at a time when the country was coming out of a long ethnic and political struggle. Agnes' household was Roman Catholic, moderately prosperous. Her parents were active aid-givers, and the children often witnessed their mother feed and shelter those in need. She was a devout churchgoer, and emphasized the importance of helping those less fortunate. The unexpected death of Agnes' father brought about a change in family fortunes, but the family continued to offer sustenance to the distressed and needy. Involvement with the Church was constant in Bojaxhiu household, and by age twelve, Agnes had decided to be a nun. She would speak very little of how this desire transpired, and it was not till she was nineteen, that her vision would begin to materialize. News in her local parish about Jesuit activities in Calcutta, conveyed the appalling conditions in which the poor and infirm lived in India. Agnes was moved by these stories. She spent her time in church activities, visiting the shrine of Madonna at Letnice (present day Kosovo, the shrine of Black Madonna) and becoming increasingly sure of her calling.

By November 1928, aged eighteen, Agnes Gonxha Bojaxhiu left Skopje to reach Paris and then Dublin, to join the Loreto Sisters (Institute of Blessed Virgin Mary). The Loreto Sisters, almost a century earlier, had branched out as a separate group under the Catholic Church. This was preceded in 1609 by English Catholic nun Mary Ward's struggle to build an independent order for women missionaries, outside male hierarchies. Religious persecution of Catholics in England and women's marginalization in church, spurred her religious activism. Built around the order of the Jesuits (Ignatius Loyola), the Loreto sisters aimed at providing free education and health services to the poor and needy, initially in Europe and later in India. Agnes enrolled in this order, and was renamed Sister Teresa after completing her novitiate period. Later, she was asked to take her vows in Darjeeling, Bengal. She was then transferred to Calcutta, the cultural and erstwhile capital of British India, a city teeming with people, facing deep impact of colonial inequities.

Sister Teresa's life in Calcutta turned out to be extraordinary from the start – for herself, the religious order she represented, and for Calcutta, a city that witnessed her relentless work for the poor, and the homeless. While Teresa had initially set out to be with the Loreto Order offering educational services for poor children, the decade of the 40s changed this. The effects of World War on the colonies, the disastrous Bengal famine of 1942–1943, Partition of Hindu India, and Calcutta's spiralling poverty, left indelible imprints on the city's landscape. In 1948, Teresa sought permission to leave the Loreto Sisters to begin her own work among the poor.

For the next few decades, Sister Teresa worked tirelessly to initiate and establish the Missionaries of Charity, under direct authority of the archbishop of Calcutta. Building homes for dying and abandoned children, lepers, thousands of destitute people, offering them care and restitution, she soon became known as Mother Teresa, a saint for the poor. From 1950 till her death in 1997, the Albanian origin Mother Teresa remained a living symbol of hope for the sick and dying in India – a saree-clad, frail, arched figure embodying the spirit of caritas. Curiously, her charitable work thrived in a Marxist state that had no links with religious evangelism. Calcutta was also where the Hindu Vedanta movement flourished. It was in Calcutta that the enormity of her work was felt, and a face of Christianity, that India had not known before. Thousands of young girls joined her mission taking religious vows, making the Missionaries of Charity a compelling social phenomenon, inspiring worldwide recognition. Eventually, it led to Teresa's beatification, in the Roman Catholic Church in 2016, nine years after her death in Calcutta. For most of India though, she was already a saint, embodied in collective imagination as a beacon of light.

Amor Dei, Amor Proximi

Much like Olivelle's interpretation of the ashrama as a mode of life adopted by an individual, Teresa's life mode was communion with the divine and life of service. She developed a religious attitude while young, but this development also coincided with other events of history. The coincidences, starting from a personal mother who was engaged in caring for the needy, a local church that impressed young minds with news of Jesuit missionaries, the Black Madonna shrine near her hometown that she visited, the creation of a missionary order exclusively for women in distant Ireland, a dream in Darjeeling, were all astonishingly synchronized with Teresa's dream, making it possible for her to pursue her calling.

Art historian Robert Freyhan writes about the dual meaning of caritas in religion, that implicates both love of God as well love of neighbor. Love of God is signified as primary, and works of mercy are considered of less value in New Testament, he notes. Hence, *Amor Dei* (love of God) and *Amor Proximi* (love of neighbor) are not the same (Freyhan, 1948, p. 68). However, the Augustinian notion of Misericordia (heartfelt experience of other's misery), could be construed closer to the notion of Caritas, Freyhan thinks, as the outward act of mercy is a sign of the indwelling Amor Dei. Sculptural panels in Hildesheim shrines in Germany suggest the notion of Caritas-Misericordia. Freyhan writes, 'On the lid of Hildesheim font, of about 1230, a figure is enthroned, surrounded by six other figures: the naked putting on a shirt, the thirsty, the sick, the prisoner looking through his iron bars, the hungry and the stranger as a pilgrim. The words of the inscription are *per opes inopem misereri*, and accordingly, the main figure is named Misericordia. She has no specific symbol, but as a center of a group of the needy, she demonstrates amor proximi according to the one scheme known to the Middle Ages, namely the six works of mercy' (Freyhan, 1948, p. 70). Freyhan concludes that this Misericordia is caritas, or amor proximi, with the aspect of amor dei remaining outside direct representation. What is signified in Teresa's story is the symbol of caritas, and its constellation in culture.

The image of Madonna of Humility, which spread widely in fourteenth century, in Italy, France, Germany and Spain, depicts something similar (Figure 6.2). The humility that is expressed in the image, and her representation in a particular emotional state of sympathetic contact with child, is evocative of Teresa. The Madonna's low posture makes her accessible to all – sinful, needy, diseased and deserted – a solicitude that characterizes her spirit of caritas. American art historian Millard Meiss notes that while humility is not among the three theological and four cardinal values in Christianity, humility is considered *radix virtutum*, from which all other virtues emerge (Meiss, 1936, p. 461). I bring the notion of caritas and humility to the story of Teresa, primarily to convey that her lifelong work in India was characterized by these traits. It was captured in a series of paintings by symbolist painter M.F. Hussain, who signified her humility and self-effacement through an erasure of her personal features, highlighting her impersonal aura in her frail, blue-rimmed saree-clad figure. A fifteenth-century tempera art of Madonna of Humility gives a similar impression of mater coelestis (Figures 6.2 and 6.3).

Teresa erased personal and subjective contents of her life in all her interviews, where she talked about her work. Instead, she stressed on the image of Christ, counting that as the most significant factor for her work among the poor. Jung had written that a conscious collective attitude can bring forth its highest expression in Christian brotherly love (Jung, 1971, para. 742). This neighborly love produces extraordinary human service, but does not reveal the personal. Instead, it manifests in the spirit of misericordia caritas in the collective. Teresa insisted that it was Christ's truth that was being revealed in her work; the contra-sexual metaphor can be discerned, but the personal, subjective contents are never in these stories. Teresa's restorative work was a sharp contrast to the material and cultural degradation that Calcutta experienced in post-independence era. The animus can emerge as a contra-sexual symbol in culture, in impersonal and objective realms, and as a compensatory phenomenon. Its manifestation may be in acts of evangelism and healing, in creative thinking, activism and welfarism. The phenomenon of the animus shows vast plurality, from dissent and disruption to empowerment and collective healing. It is also revealed in one-sided pursuit of goals and sometimes, in solitary, independent living.

FIGURE 6.2 Virgin of Humility.

Source: Fra Angelico, Public domain, via Wikimedia Commons, https://commons.wikimedia.
org/wiki/File:Virgen_humildad-fra_angelico.jpg

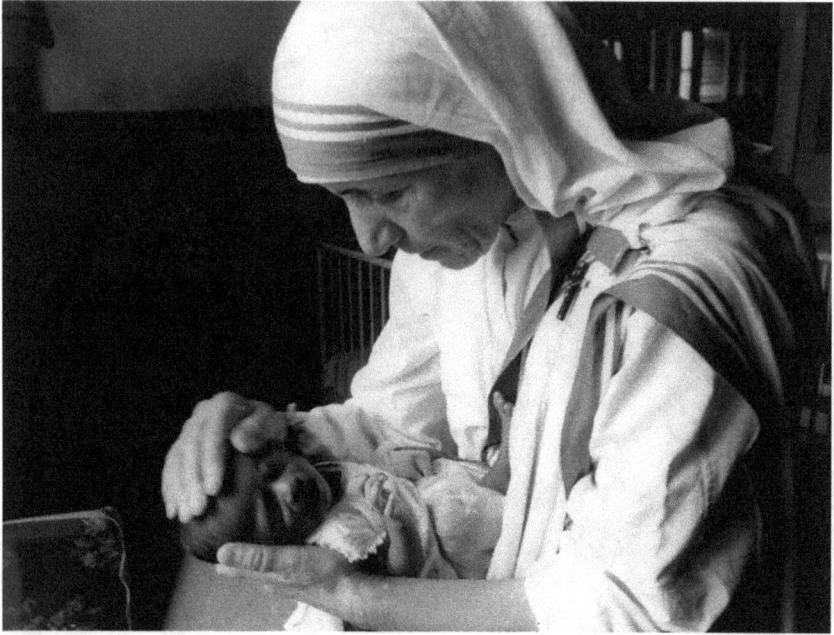

FIGURE 6.3 Mother Teresa.

Source: ZUMA Press, Inc./Alamy Stock Photo.

Credit: Keystone Pictures, USA /ZUMAPRESS.com /Alamy Live News.

References

Brooke, R. (2015) *Jung and Phenomenology*. London: Routledge.

Coward, H. (1985) 'Jung and Kundalini', *Journal of Analytical Psychology*, 30(4), pp. 379–392.

Dourley, J. (1995) 'The Religious Implications of Jung's Psychology', *Journal of Analytical Psychology*, 40, pp. 177–203.

Eliade, M. (1958) *Yoga, Immortality and Freedom*, Translated from French by Willard R. Trask, Bollingen Series LVI. Princeton, NJ: Princeton University Press.

Fordham, M. (1975) 'Memories and Thoughts about C.G. Jung', *Journal of Analytical Psychology*, 20, pp. 102–113.

Freyhan, R. (1948) 'The Evolution of the Caritas Figure in the Thirteenth and Fourteenth Centuries', *Journal of the Warburg and Courtauld Institutes*, 11, pp. 68–86.

Greene, M. (2004) *Mother Teresa: A Biography*. Westport, CT: Greenwood Press.

Jones, R. (2020) 'The Snake in the Mandala: Dialogical Aspects of Jung's "A Study in the Process of Individuation"', *Journal of Analytical Psychology*, 65(2), pp. 389–407.

Jung, C. G. (1950) *The Symbolic Life*, Vol. 18, The Collected Works of C.G. Jung. Princeton: Princeton University Press.

Jung, C. G. (1969) *The Structure and Dynamics of the Psyche*, Vol. 8, The Collected Works of C.G. Jung. Princeton: Princeton University Press.

Jung, C. G. (1971) *Psychological Types*, Vol. 6, The Collected Works of C.G. Jung. Princeton: Princeton University Press.

Jung, C. G. (1989) *Memories, Dreams, Recollections*. Recorded and edited by Angela Jaffe. New York: Vintage Books.

Jung, C. G. (1996) *The Psychology of Kundalini Yoga, Notes of the Seminar Given in 1932 by C.G. Jung*. Edited by S. Shamdasani. Bollingen Series XCIX. Princeton, NJ: Princeton University Press.

Jung, C. G. (2009) *The Red Book: Liber Novus*. Edited by Sonu Shamdasani. New York: W.W. Norton.

Meiss, M. (1936) 'The Madonna of Humility', *The Art Bulletin*, 18(4), pp. 435–465.

Odajnyk, W. (2004) 'The Archetypal Interpretation of Fairy Tales: Bluebeard', *Psychological Perspectives*, 47(2), 247–275.

Olivelle, P. (1993) *The Ashrama System: The History and Hermeneutics of a Religious Institution*. New York: Oxford University Press.

Owens, L. S. and Hoeller, S. (2014) 'Carl Gustav Jung and The Red Book: Liber Novus'. In Leeming, D. (ed.), *Encyclopedia of Psychology and Religion*. 2nd ed. New York, Heidelberg, Dordrecht, and London: Springer Reference.

Perrault, C. (1697/1977) 'Bluebeard'. In A. Lang (ed.), *Popular Tales*. New York: Arno Press. Available at Project Gutenberg at https://www.gutenberg.org/files/33931/33931-h/33931-h.htm.

Redfearn, J. W. T. (1977) 'The Self and Individuation', *Journal of Analytical Psychology*, 22(2), pp. 125–141.

Skar, P. (2004) 'Chaos and Self-Organization: Emergent Patterns at Critical Life Transitions', *Journal of Analytical Psychology*, 49(2), pp. 243–262.

Tagore, R. (2016) *Swarabitan*, Vol. 60, Visva Bharati, India.

Zinkin, L. (2008) 'Your Self: Did You Find It or Did You Make It?' *Journal of Analytical Psychology*, 53, pp. 389–406.

7

CONCLUSION

Tracing the Animus

In the preceding chapters, the phenomenology of the animus was traced in psyche and culture, in personal and objective realms. The feminine psyche was the primary realm in which the animus was examined. Multiple images, myths and lived experiences were brought in to explore nuances of contra-sexuality. Although the feminine encompasses a diverse range of experiences for those who identify as women, the animus, draws our attention to emotions, feelings and fantasies that are evoked in relation to the contra-sexual other. The other could be masculinist forces of culture in opposition to the feminine, or contrarian impulses within the psyche, of unconscious masculine. The narratives showed how the psyche responded in unexpected ways when confronted with contra-sexual otherness, the image of the other being central in catalyzing new behaviors. The unconscious contents that emerge are not assimilated easily; they are approached in instinctive ways at first. The conscious ego is challenged by the unconscious, and an inner opposition prevails between conscious and unconscious forces. The psyche undergoes numerous conflicts and tensions before contra-sexual impulses are incorporated into consciousness, or related with meaningfully. The narratives captured these dynamics of otherness, in personal, social, cultural and religious realms. More importantly, it placed the phenomena of the animus in culture, wider histories of knowledge, transcultural narratives, lived experiences, and synchronicity, for understanding the complexity and nuances of the archetype.

The animus was found constellated in culture against dark and destructive masculinist forces. In the preceding narratives, we found that patriarchal

DOI: 10.4324/9780429423727-7

dominance was countered through dissent and subversion, and in radical reinstatement of the feminine. Like the trope of the mythic Durga in Bengal, the psyche adopts a combative attitude against perceived threats, and in extreme cases, attempts to annihilate the other. The phenomenon of the animus was seen to be active in social and personal worlds when there was a repression of the feminine.

The other is a familiar stranger in the psyche. Ontological otherness can be discerned in inner figures and outer, in familiar otherness, or in the distant and exotic other. 'Logically, this relationship could cover a wide range of possibilities, from opposition to complementary, from difference, separation, distinction to alternative, remaining, supplementary' (Papadopoulos, 2002, p. 165). The other is central in denoting psyche's contra-sexuality, but is not symbolized in inner worlds alone. It is found in cultural forces, synchronistic events and in history. We witnessed the other in Phoolan's journey, and in Dopdi's bodily rebellion. We saw it in Bharti's poise and agency, and discerned it in Teresa, in her pursuit of a spiritual goal and the long passage she undertook to find her calling. Their radical choices, dissents and life-paths stemmed from within, as also from culture. Papadopoulos writes that opposites are related, and the other, despite its inherent oppositionality, is part of a larger whole. Paul Ricoeur's deliberation that there is no Self without the other is relevant to note, he concurs.

While the antecedents of the animus may be in individual telos, psyche's interaction with the environment is crucial in shaping its emergent contents. Across narratives, we found that the constellation of the contra-sexual other in the feminine psyche took place in contexts where oppositional forces were active. The other was constellated in instances of sameness, as was the case of Bharti and Priya. Their seeming unity veiled the otherness of caste, class, identity, emotion and thinking. Inner duality was experienced in social and ideological differences, and in oppositions in personality. The emergence of contra-sexual animus in the psyche symbolized an initiation and the beginning of an individuation process. The individual's relation to the collective was critical in shaping the contours of this journey. Tagore's remark that the individual could not be submerged under the collective, and Jung's observation that collective values were in dialectical relation with individual consciousness, are pertinent here. In narratives of the feminine, writers Mahasweta Devi, Adrienne Rich, Wendy Doniger and Jael Silliman were impelled by the unknown in their pursuit of creative paths. Their journeys took them beyond normative gender worlds. Contra-sexual energies were channeled in critical inquiries and radical acts, instead of being utilized in domesticity, motherhood, marriage or companionship. The latter was Jung's essentialist approach to feminine as Eros and its place in the collective, where he said, the masculine impulse of the animus could not be exteriorized. But in turning unknown and irrational creative desires outward, not only was new consciousness generated by these feminists, but there also occurred radical questioning of collective ethos and its inherent prejudices. In the final count, the individual's goal of consciousness is not just for bringing about transformation in the personal, but also, transformation of the collective.

The emergent psyche, imbued with the spirit of animus, displayed multiplicity of character – from animistic, chthonic, energies and antagonism, to capacity for thinking, differentiation, discernment and self-agency, with potential for transcendence and transformation. Self-actualization was key; the animus showed radicalness, even in spiritual acts. Mother Teresa's arduous journey that preceded her founding of a religious order, contained seeds of a radical feminine self, that could navigate cultural other, in differences of ethnicity, language, religion, history and political affairs. Although the animus may be accompanied by inchoate and aggravated emotions in the beginning, it can hold a goal-oriented telos. The unconscious animus manifests in anarchist impulses as well as in healing acts, the catalyzing factor in these journeys being the image of a contra-sexual other. Even in Christiana Morgan, the dominant forces of her individuation journey were the contra-sexual figures of her father, analyst or lover.

The attributes of masculine and feminine in narratives of the animus were found to be fluid and mutating, ranging from dark, destructive, demonic emotions to creative, empathetic and affirmative drives. Rohan's coming-of-age struggle was against an authoritarian, father, whose personality was diametrically opposite his, in contra-sexual undertones of masculine and feminine. A diverse psychological spectrum of the animus was envisioned in the narratives, from feminine articulation, shrewdness, self-assurance, healing to rage and aspiration. When the feminine was found to be, self-driven and assured, its contra-sexual other was fickle and unsure – as was the case with Bharti and Priya. When collective behaviors of the feminine were centered around submission and docility, in Phoolan it surfaced in unusual fierceness, compensating the collective attitude. The young bride in the myth of the bluebeard man, oblivious of the dangers awaiting her, the naive and confused Priya, and the guileless Parvati who playfully models a child out of clay, are goaded by feminine innocence and inexperience, as they encounter the dark and disruptive other.

When constellated, the animus is seen to cohere both thinking and feeling, discrimination and empathy, as was the case of Sister Teresa, an ordinary religious novitiate who found ingenious ways to fructify her mission in a strange land. Opposites were constellated in these encounters, and the individual was imbued with unusual strength and ability. Teresa's saintly persona was a contrast to the starving, emaciated, diseased and dying bodies that she held close to her. Bharti's self-assured demeanor were a contrast to Priya's fickleness. Phoolan's militant attitude was a deviation from dominant feminine behavior in her milieu. When she took on a powerful male lobby, she was raped, crushed and branded an outlaw. The narratives showed that the animus had distinctive telos and purpose. If the notion of the feminine was located in maternal, domestic and personal relations in one-sided ways, or in Eros and feeling, the eruption of the unconscious animus would be in expressions of independence, radical thinking and creativity, restorative and regenerative acts in the collective and intellectual flowering, that countered collective perceptions.

Contextualizing the Animus

History

The phenomenology of the animus in this volume has been explored in the realm of culture and history. Aside from nuances of the contra-sexual psyche that were discerned because of historical positioning, such an approach also reveals how Jung's psychological constructs are reflected across cultures in difference and similarity. The western empirical concept of the unconscious is distinct from philosophical tenets of consciousness, in India. Jung's unresolved conversations with Indian philosophers on the notion of supra-consciousness and the nature of psychological unconscious signify the cultural other (Sengupta, 2013). The foregoing chapters revealed that the impulse for transcultural dialogue in science, philosophy, religion and history has existed from early on, despite feelings of otherness, or perhaps because of it. Jung was not the first in history to initiate dialogues with India, although he was the first psychoanalyst to have done so.

Synchronicity

Since the notion of the psychological unconscious is absent in Indian thought, the historical context becomes important for understanding why an inquiry on the animus is initiated, with focus on culture. How do we bridge an alien psychology with the lived context of India, vastly dissimilar from Jung's European environment? From examining history, we know that eastern notions about mind, Self, consciousness, death and afterlife have very little equivalences in western empirical psychology. Unexpected and improbable historical coincidences aligned western scholars with Indian culture, bringing unrelated cultural contents and personalities in interaction with each other. I have named these acausal links as synchronicities of culture, or meaningful coincidences between cultural worlds. The dream of the book titled 'Animus' also emerged from such cultural synchronicity. Although, Jung's inquiries on India took place at a time of western cultural dominance, with views such as the 'savage other' in circulation, his interface opened up inquiries about the psyche, in eastern realms. With increasing scrutiny about colonialist and hegemonic biases in western psychological theories and their universalist assumptions, Jung's links with India affirm an alternate worldview. Whatever his reservations about the psychological impact of cross-cultural journeys, such inquiries have been part of history, and continue to thrive even today. Locating Jung's work in India has implications for transdisciplinary studies, in containing universalist assumptions about the unconscious, and affirming the role of cultural specificities.

Culture

Tracing the phenomenology of the animus in culture implies that the contrasexual archetype has constituents beyond the personal. The cultural constituents of the animus are highlighted in various ways – in the myth of the goddess which is ritually enacted in a collective, in Dopdi's seditious moves as a disenfranchised farm laborer, in Bharti's oppressed feminine self as a young Dalit lesbian, and in Phoolan's extreme oppression and vulnerability in a caste-ridden, misogynist society – in all of them cultural attributes are identified and articulated. Cultural contexts are also highlighted in Rich's and Morgan's life stories, their social and political environments, all of which go beyond personal inner worlds.

The sentient memories of the goddess described in Chapter 3 are distinct, for example, from Wendy Doniger's memories of the goddess festival in Calcutta, which she witnessed as a young student during her Indian sojourn. The cacophonic, disordered, brutish performative rituals that Doniger saw are closer to Jung's experience of Kali temples in India, lined with blood, chaos and dirt (Doniger, 2022, pp. 145–148). Jung perceived this as the alien psyche of the east, whose contents are foreign to us, like the inhabitants of the house who live with us, but are not us (Jung, 1966; Jung, 1989). While memories of the goddess evoked in me images of a numinous and incandescent feminine, for Doniger, witnessing the pagan rituals and surrounding mayhem was a disquieting experience. Doniger's view is a useful addition, highlighting the profanity that surrounds the sacred. It is elaborated also by Indian historian Tapati Guha-Thakurta in 'In the Name of the Goddess', where she describes the reduction of the religious and the sacred in the commodification of the myth, during the annual goddess festival. The festival is celebrated through cacophonous music and broadcasts, accumulation of city's debris and waste, garish posters and commercial displays, and in general disorder and commotion, revealing the dark side of a sacred ritual (Guha-Thakurta, 2015). Doniger compares the nightlong invocations of the goddess with incantations of Midnight Mass celebrations, while Guha-Thakurta presents an array of images that highlights the festival's secular structure, showing how it transforms into an industry during the festival period, providing scarce employment to many, and boosting its economy.

Subjectivity shapes our notion of culture as much as our location in culture shapes our subjective worlds. The subjective contents of Shiva and Parvati's myth are different from the mystical union portrayed in the image of *Ardhanarishvara* (half-man, half-woman). The mythic contents are more dynamic and disruptive than the outer image. Together, they form a composite whole. The myth of the bluebeard man, shows an unconscious contrasexual image – a man's compulsive desire for destroying the feminine, seen also in the collective psyche in Phoolan's village. Her transformation occurred from within the same collective – both dark and light coalesce to form a whole. Reflections of the goddess similarly reveal both the transcendent and irreligious, secular and holy, intimate and alien. Contra-sexual opposition is not only in relation to the personal, but implicated also in wider cultural forces. Adrienne Rich's gendered alterity and radical affirmation of the feminine self, emerged from her opposition to collective ideology. The Self is shaped from cultural grounds as well as personal, and from psyche's dialectical and oppositional relation with the other. It becomes important to identify the diverse personal and cultural constituents of the animus in understanding its emergence.

The Self

The Self is symbolized as a dynamic concept in the yogachakras. The opposing and reconciling movements within the chakras show an interactive field between various objects – a snake, phallic stone, yoni, lotus, earth and seven-tusked elephant. A complex, self-organizing process is symbolized where the contents change form till an iridescent, illuminated radiance appears. The serpent reconciles various kinds of dualities as it ascends the chakras. The Self's ability to encounter the other, engage in opposition and find coherent meaning, with potential for further change, is emphasized in the chakra symbology.

The phenomenon of the animus shows similar dispositions in the narratives, where chaotic and irrational impulses change into more synergized mental states. The trajectory of the animus involves a composite whole, in contents that are fluid and transformative. Inferior thinking and tendency to impersonate masculine behavior are not the only identifiable traits of feminine contra-sexuality. The contra-sexual other stirs up alien and contrasting behaviors in the self, and these are not only of mimetic value. The animus reveals distinctive telos in feminine trajectories. This becomes clearer in the life modes adopted by women, in journeys that are radical and inventive, like the image of the Gradiva. Jung talked about conscious one-sidedness, and these journeys reflect a one-sidedness. Jung said that a conscious capacity for one-sidedness is a sign of sophistry, but involuntary one-sidedness is barbaric (Jung, 1971, para 346).

The psyche does not transition through life stages in expected and conventional ways in such instances, from worldly life to retreat and reflection, or from marriage and domesticity to retirement, as outlined in the ashrama. Writer Mahasweta Devi deliberated at length about the feelings of loss she experienced when she embarked on an independent life, leaving behind her marriage and her young son (Kishore, 2016). The impulse to pursue a creative idea fuels feminine choice, a specific life-mode, a surrender to it even, and acceptance of trials and tribulations. The feminine self is always in flux in these journeys, constantly in the making. In a popular Baul song the Self is described as ephemeral and elusive, forever around, waiting to be discovered, but never quite grasped.

In a mystic ocean, I found my beloved –
A numinous, golden being.
I have waited for it, and wondered about our meeting –
But it would not be mine,
Even when I felt it was, and tried to hold it close.

Feminine Emancipatory Journeys

The phenomenon of the animus has wider, emancipatory resonance. The image of three young women from the east who converged in the distant United States in the late-nineteenth century to receive medical education, pioneering women's foray into medicine, is a stirring reminder of the intellectual impulse of the feminine psyche. Anandibai Joshee, Keiko Okai and Sabat Islambouli, Indian, Japanese and Syrian by birth, ventured into medical studies in distant America when women had not yet attained the right to vote and when education was still taboo for women. Anandibai (1865–1887) was steered by an eccentric, willful husband and by her own experience of losing her child at birth as a teenaged mother – an event that, she said, reflected the pathetic condition of women's health in nineteenth-century colonial India. Given her meagre resources she would have let her medical dream die, but a series of synchronicities steered her admission into the first American medical college for women, from where she graduated along with Okai and Islambouli. Anandibai endured a traumatic childhood, an abusive husband, impoverishment, social isolation and a debilitating health condition in her short lifespan. Despite these travails, the dream for an egalitarian world fueled her journey, underscoring a radical, creative feminine impetus – creativity that Jung described as being innate only to men. Sociologist Meera Kosambi traces Anandibai's iconic passage to the west in a life fragmented between opposites, in a world where women were deeply marginalized and discriminated. Anandibai documented many of these conditions of women in her correspondences with her mentor, which Kosambi accessed in reconstructing her history (Kosambi, 1996). The contextualization of the animus in post-Jungian discourse has to take into account these early histories, pioneering feminist acts and its particular telos in the social world (Figure 7.1).

FIGURE 7.1   Women in Science – 1885.

Source: Women's Medical College of Pennsylvania Photograph Collection in Drexel University Archival Collection, https://commons.wikimedia.org/wiki/File:Anandibai_Joshee,_Kei_Okami,_and_Tabat_M._Islambooly.jpg

Archetypal, Personal and Collective

As historical instances and narratives in this volume show, individuals imbibe collective ideals in their gender orientations and identities. The radical feminine makes a deliberate and concerted move away from these collective values. This places the psyche in direct conflict with the collective. Whether in hostility or alliance, the environment critically shapes the Self. The relation between the unconscious psyche and the collective is interwoven in many ways.

Christiana Morgan's struggle to find meaning in her visionary outpourings contains an inclination towards the archetypal, which she believed was the right ground for nurturing her creative life. In an incisive account of narrative love stories in history, clinical psychologist Ruthellen Josselson deconstructs the relationship of Henry Murray and Christiana Morgan, drawing facts from two esteemed biographies, about a love that was difficult to name because it was neither a conventional affair nor a social pact. Josselson writes, 'Relationships between two people are always triadic', as social context is always implicated, in a real, practical world (Josselson, 2007, p. 21).

According to biographical notes from the two volumes, Morgan rarely let the outer context of family and social world interrupt her inner life, but Murray experienced proverbial guilt, fear and anxiety about his extra-marital liaison(s), while at Harvard. Taking cue from Jung during her analysis with him, Morgan understood archetypal constellations of the unconscious anima in men, and was inspired to play the role of Murray's muse (and anima). She wanted to place their love in an exalted, timeless, visionary frame. The couple christened themselves as Wona and Mansol, emphasizing the mythical nature of their relationship, where Christiana's visionary imagination, passion and unconventional beliefs fueled Murray's creative and emotional core, and stirred his life energies. They embarked on writing a *Proposition,* a living record of their relation, engaging in various naming rituals, believing that their love had the potential to transform the world. Yet, the couple struggled to contextualize it, Josselson writes, and the relation swayed between Morgan's need for intimacy and attention and Murray's bouts of neglect and absence. It swung between extremes, with unconventional experimentation and volatility characterizing some of its contents. It was fueled by a passion for the mystical and symbolic, in one-sided ways, about whose pitfalls Jung had written (Jung, 1969, para 277).

Contra-sexual relations are evolved in lived contexts, in their struggles in ordinary, practical worlds. From the numinous syzygy in a dream recounted earlier where the image of a transcendental union was offset by the earthy, grounded spirit of village folk, the mystical longing that Shiva and Parvati feel for each other which are channeled in their dialectical encounters, to the silent affinity between Dopdi and Dulna, that is rooted in their revolutionary spirit, the lived context of contra-sexual relations, is critical for its coherence. The feminine Self is not formed without necessary trials and tribulations in its relation with the other. The phenomena of the animus include multiple subjectivities and contexts, archetypal, personal and collective, social and political interests, their relativization in lived experience, rather than only personal subjectivity.

The Significance or Insignificance of the Archetypal

Transdisciplinary scholar Stephen Frosh writes that the psychosocial is a formative area of study that encompasses social and personal. Its relevance lies in the fact that it has not become reified into a fixed discipline. Transdisciplinarity unsettles subject boundaries, while precariously holding together contradictions and differences. In psychosocial, it emphasizes personal experience, reflexivity, ethics, intersubjectivity, embodiment, affect, theorizing from the realm of ordinary experience, and deliberating on the notion of the other (Frosh, Vyrgioti and Walsh, 2022). Such an approach attempts to look at imbalances of history, race, violence and gender through the realm of the unconscious.

Frosh's approach of psychosocial aligns well with the contents of the narratives in this volume, except that it does not foreground culture and unconscious, archetypes, myths, religious metaphors and subaltern perspectives. Its theoretical framework is in critical theory, that is detached from colonial histories and indigenous knowledge, although Frosh is keen to offset this in future research. Further still, psychoanalysis as a western disciplinary domain, historically centered around wealthy, upper-class clients, has a fundamental disconnect with non-western cultures. This volume foregrounds culture to bridge these theoretical and contextual gaps, using Jung's concept of archetypes as a vital construct that links discrete and dissimilar worlds. As Renos Papadopoulos has written, 'The Other-as-Archetype represents the pinnacle of Jung's theoretical endeavors as it offers a structuring principle which is also connected with broader cultural and societal perspectives' (Papadopoulos, 2002, p. 170). The narratives take this notion forward by deconstructing archetypes and locating differences of experience, instead of emphasizing universality of the psyche.

In re-envisioning Jung's original view of the contra-sexual animus, the social and cultural have been brought centerstage in this work, since notions of masculine and feminine have their underpinnings in social worlds, and are shaped by perceptions of gender in culture. As Judith Butler says, 'To be a gender, whether man, woman, or otherwise, is to be engaged in an ongoing cultural interpretation of bodies and, hence, to be dynamically positioned within a field of cultural possibilities' (Butler, 1986, p. 36). Biological gender differences are rendered with social and cultural meanings, and across cultures this is denoted in specific ways. This renders the animus with multiple meanings. Butler says, 'In other words, to be a woman is to become a woman; it is not a matter of acquiescing to a fixed ontological status, in which case one could be born a woman, but, rather, an active process of appropriating, interpreting and reinterpreting received cultural possibilities' (Butler, 1986, p. 36). The essence of the feminine is derived from a composite realm of psyche, history, culture, religion, myth and science, instead of an a priori feminine. Jung's descriptions do not bring the cultural context of the feminine and lived experience into focus, but this, in the formative stages of psychology, in his time, is understandable.

Jung described animus constellations as problematic, especially when exteriorized. Contra-sexual symbols and descriptions in cultural narratives show that the animus has purposive and individuating goals, even if its expression is chaotized and incoherent initially. The psyche develops self-reflexivity and discernment as it evolves, which Jung himself suggested is the goal of individuation. The animus has transformative potential, and its one-sidedness, obduracy and dissentious spirit are integral to it. For all its varied manifestations and qualities, its core is mystical, with its significance and meaning emerging only in lived contexts. I propose that the entire trajectory be taken into view in viewing the animus, rather than specific behaviors encountered in the personal.

Jung viewed the masculine animus in feminine psyche as largely an irreconcilable duality, prone to producing psychic distortions. But images of the animus in cultural narratives show that contra-sexual otherness induces new contents of the unconscious psyche to emerge, and triggers developmental journeys. These journeys contain painful initiations and descents, as also vital self-knowledge and self-actualization. The contra-sexual other is catalytic and germinal for the psyche. In contra-sexual pairing, the pull of opposites and intimations of wholeness fuel erotic attractions. Having fluid and interchangeable psychological traits allows fluid and dynamic contra-sexual relations to flow. The redundancy of the archetype is in defining it with fixed meanings, emphasizing its primordial or universal essence, and viewing it as a philosophical or metaphysical construct, instead of empirical.

Psychological and Cultural Elements of the Animus

In 'Contemporary Perspectives in Jungian Analysis', Joseph Cambray and Linda Carter discuss analytic methods developed by Jung and share the theoretical underpinnings of Jungian analysis (Cambray and Carter, 2004). Jung's emphasis on dreams and image, use of active imagination, amplification, transference and counter-transference evolved an emergentist model of the Self, that was distinct from Freud's methods. The authors highlight how Jung's central concept of individuation separates his methods from Freud's, and how the Jungian approach draws on multidisciplinary fields to have a fuller view of psychic reality. Jung distinguished between notions of ego and Self – the first, a conscious standpoint of the psyche, and the latter, a notion of wholeness that includes both conscious and unconscious contents. Individuation as a psychological maturation process where the individual develops his or her unique potential, separate from collective ideals, finds a relationship with the world without surrendering to collectivity, was Jung's central proposal about the psyche. Cambray and Carter highlight the precision needed for employing techniques of amplification and active imagination in analysis, underscoring at the same time, the importance of using cultural material for accessing unconscious contents.

Jung's deliberations about the psyche have an empirical basis, as Cambray and Carter elaborate, evolved from his therapeutic experience, early scientific studies, cultural scholarship and academic collaborations. My exposition of the phenomenology of the animus is from within the lived experience of a culture, its myths, politics, history, knowledge, social stratification, whose antecedents are old and whose intricacies are distinct from Jung's western world. Although post-Jungian scholars have demystified and deconstructed many of Jung's original notions about the animus, what I present here is a synopsis of the main strands of the animus in Jung's theory, and cultural variations and extensions that I found in myths, symbols, narratives, history and lived contexts. The differences are sometimes striking, but more importantly, the cultural impressions compel us to view the phenomenon of contra-sexuality with a wider lens than the way originally envisioned. For a comparison of Jung's views about the animus and parallel Indian concepts, see Table 7.1

In 'Political and Clinical Developments of Analytical Psychology', Jungian analyst Andrew Samuels deliberates on the expansion of Jungian psychotherapy in non-western worlds and its implications for Jungian theory and practice (Samuels, 2014). Samuels' focus is on the therapeutic domain, its racist legacies and false eulogizing of Jung's ideas, insulation from culture and politics, and economic disparities in the field that continue to keep therapeutic practice limited to elitist domains. The theme of culture opens up questions about Jung's involvement with oriental scholarship, colonial legacies, not to mention the contents of some of the early texts themselves, that are elitist and misogynist in tenor. But Jung bridged disparate and contrasting domains of psychology and religion, archaic and contemporary, which few even attempted in mainstream psychology. He expressed cultural ambivalences instead of universalizing all experiences and opened up possibilities for cultures to enter into dialogues about the unconscious. Samuels

TABLE 7.1 Animus – Psychological and Cultural Dimensions

Jung's Expositions of the Animus	Cultural Comparisons and Extensions
Jung defined the animus as a contra-sexual archetype, i.e. a secondary muted unconscious gender under a dominant and identifiable gender orientation.	No theoretical articulation of anima and animus in Indian texts. Ample evidence of contra-sexual symbols and imagery in cultural narratives.
Repressed contents of the psyche erupt as autonomous complexes in the individual. The unconscious contra-sexual other is hidden, muted and repressed, evoked through individuals of opposite gender.	Psychological notion of the unconscious absent in Indian thought. Notions of ego, Self, anima, animus, shadow, complexes have their parallels in culture, but there are no theoretical expositions of these in Indian knowledge. Concepts of self, consciousness, emotions, mind, *gunas* are found in Indian philosophy.
Jung's contra-sexual archetype interiorizes gender binaries, with masculine and feminine functioning as conscious and unconscious elements of the individual psyche. Jung did not consider social phenomena as important for describing concept of contra-sexuality.	Indian myths signify masculine and feminine in binary gender symbols. Instances of gender fluidity are also seen. Social theories categorize gender as culturally constructed, operating within patriarchal frames. Unconscious gender is not theorized in Indian thought.
Jung proposed individuation as a process for integrating these psychic dualities. This means bringing the masculine animus into conscious reflection in the feminine psyche.	Cultural and social approaches ask for a reformulation of gender notions, removal of biases and reinstatement of equity and equality.
Jung located the feminine in Eros and the masculine in Logos in fixed and unchanging ways.	Myths provide contra-sexual symbolization, androgynous imagery and notions of gender fluidity. Notion of wholeness is proposed in Indian philosophy
Jung's characterization of the animus in feminine psyche locates it as problematic, with false adoption of masculine traits, and irrational thinking and emotions dominating animus behavior. Jung did not delve into the socio-cultural world and its inbuilt imbalances. His emphasis was on the archetypal aspect of	Cultural narratives note feminine potency. Ascendent feminine motifs like Kali or Durga are celebrated in culture. Both Eros and Logos are implicated in feminine myths, Logos is attached to masculine and Eros to feminine. Contemporary narratives, describe feminine subjectivity through social and political contexts of gender discrimination.

contra-sexuality. Emphasis on gender in India is on socio-cultural constructs.

Jung's view was that the feminine psyche cannot identify itself with the archetype of the masculine animus, and dissociate itself from Eros.

Jung's concept of the contra-sexual animus gave importance to its archetypal significance and did not include the historical context of gender, or how masculine and feminine are shaped in culture.

Jung viewed contra-sexual archetypes exclusively in personal and therapeutic realms.

Jung's concept of the animus and contra-sexual psyche identifies oppositions within the psyche, that are intrinsic to psychological life.

Jung's ideas are flawed by their essentialist biases, disconnect from environment, and need contemporary revisioning.

Both approaches of social and psychological, are aligned in this volume.

Eros and Logos are signified in principles like Ida-Pingala, Purusha-Prakriti, etc. They signify oppositional qualities, not necessarily always linked to binary gender.

In contemporary cultural narratives, the feminine is portrayed as radical and potent force.

Cultural narratives deploy feminine metaphors of combat, resilience, dissent, protest, healing and regeneration as elements of feminine subjectivity, and capture the changing dynamics of gender in contemporary history.

Narratives about feminine subjectivity locate its dynamics in personal, as well as in social, in lived history, religion, politics, myth, suggesting a psychoid basis for the archetype.

Narratives about the feminine are found in a variety of cultural contents. They expand the notion of feminine, with psychological, social, archetypal aspects brought in interaction with each other. Cultural specificities show the animus in radical, transformative, individuating nuances.

anticipates the evolution of an interdisciplinary Jungian psychology that will not be colonized by established concepts, that will entertain the alien as part of one's inner alienness, and tie current political and environmental predicaments to therapeutic dialogues. The disruptive narratives in this volume, the animus as a contra-sexual entity that bridges psyche and culture, shows an emergent new analytical psychology, envisioned in a transdisciplinary framework. Its provisional and fluid nature is a reflection of the ways in which Jung's ideas are being re-envisioned today in an uncertain, ambivalent world. Such re-envisioning challenges universalist approaches to the psyche, expands on Jung's original ideas in including the other, deliberates on problematic aspects of history, the racial, sexual, gendered, ethnic and religious other, and locates depth psychology within an inclusive worldview.

References

Butler, J. (1986) 'Sex and Gender in Simone de Beauvoir's *Second Sex*', *Yale French Studies*, 72, pp. 35–49.

Cambray, J. and Carter, L. (2004) 'Analytic Methods Revisited' in Cambray, J. and Carter, L. (eds.), *Analytical Psychology: Contemporary Perspectives in Jungian Analysis*. New York: Brunner-Routledge, pp. 116–148.

Doniger, W. (2022) *An American Girl in India: Letters and Recollections, 1963–64*. New Delhi: Speaking Tiger Books.

Frosh, S., Vyrgioti, M., and Walsh, J. (2022) 'Handbook of Psychosocial Studies Introduction' in Frosh, S., Vyrgioti, M., and Walsh, J. (eds.), *The Palgrave Handbook of Psychosocial Studies*. Cham, Switzerland: Palgrave Macmillan, pp. 1–12.

Guha-Thakurta, T. (2015) *In the Name of the Goddess: The Durga Pujas of Kolkata*. New Delhi: Primus Books.

Josselson, R. (2007) 'Love in the Narrative Context: The Relationship between Henry Murray and Christiana Morgan' in Josselson, R., Lieblich, A., and McAdams, D. P. (eds.), *The Meaning of Others: Narrative Studies of Relationships*. Washington, DC: American Psychological Association, pp. 21–49.

Jung, C. G. (1966) *Two Essays in Analytical Psychology*, Vol. 7, The Collected Works of C. G. Jung. 2nd ed. Princeton, NJ: Princeton University Press.

Jung, C. G. (1969) *The Archetypes and the Collective Unconscious*, Vol. 9, pt. 1, The Collected Works of C. G. Jung. Princeton, NJ: Princeton University Press.

Jung, C. G. (1971) *Psychological Types*, Vol. 6, The Collected Works of C. G. Jung. 2nd ed. Princeton, NJ: Princeton University Press.

Jung, C. G. (1989) *Memories, Dreams, Recollections*. Recorded and edited by Angela Jaffe. New York: Vintage Books.

Kishore, N. (2016) 'Talking Writing: Four Conversations with Mahasweta Devi', YouTube video, The Seagull Foundation for the Arts, January 14, https://www.seagullindia.com/wordpress1/talking-writing-four-conversations-with-mahasweta-devi.

Kosambi, M. (1996) 'Anandibai Joshee: Retrieving a Fragmented Feminist Image', *Economic and Political Weekly*, 31(49), pp. 3189–3197.

Papadopoulos, R. K. (2002) 'The Other Other: When the Exotic Other Subjugates the Familiar Other', *Journal of Analytical Psychology*, 47, pp. 163–188.

Samuels, A. (2014) 'Political and Clinical Developments in Analytical Psychology, 1972–2014: Subjectivity, Equality and Diversity – Inside and Outside the Consulting Room', *Journal of Analytical Psychology*, 59(5), pp. 641–660.

Sengupta, S. (2013) *Jung in India*. New Orleans, LA: Spring Journal Books.

INDEX

For Product Safety Concerns and Information please contact our EU
representative GPSR@taylorandfrancis.com
Taylor & Francis Verlag GmbH, Kaufingerstraße 24, 80331 München, Germany

www.ingramcontent.com/pod-product-compliance
Lightning Source LLC
Chambersburg PA
CBHW070345270326
41926CB00017B/3994